LIVING WITH THE
ALGORITHM:
SERVANT OR MASTER?

AI GOVERNANCE AND POLICY
FOR THE FUTURE

Tim Clement-Jones
With the assistance of
Coran Darling

UNICORN

First published by Unicorn
an imprint of Unicorn Publishing Group, 2024
Charleston Studio
Meadow Business Centre
Lewes BN8 5RW

www.unicornpublishing.org

ISBN 978-1-911397-92-2

Cover design by Unicorn
Typeset by Vivian Head

Printed by Short Run Press, Exeter, UK

Contents

'We should regulate AI before it regulates us'
Yuval Noah Harari[1]

Preface

Over the past few years, we have begun to see an emerging divergence across the world in how countries, governments, and organisations are approaching the development and deployment of artificial intelligence, often fuelled by strongly held views on whether the technology poses a systemic risk to humanity as a whole or not. A cursory glance at public initiatives such as the development of targeted regulation, and international events and campaigns such as the open letter from AI experts calling for a pause on development of AI in May 2023,[2] demonstrates that consensus on approach is far from being achieved and governance of the technology is very much in a fragmented state. One of the most pressing current questions across all sectors and industries is whether society waits until the existential risks of AI become more apparent before implementing tailored measures, or whether we approach AI with more immediate intervention as existing and developing risks are identified.

The intention of this book is to bring together a practical framework which distils many of the key insights from these approaches. I have set out both where I believe material risks continue to pose substantial – yes, and in some cases existential – risks to individuals and organisations and also the form of regulatory intervention which I believe will foster the creativity of developers and innovators, while mitigating many of the current known and future unknown risks posed by AI and AI-leveraged technology.

As someone heavily involved in AI policy for many years, I continue to believe in the importance of law and regulation and effective policy initiatives for ensuring that AI is developed and deployed in ways that offer greater societal benefit and less potential harm. Given the relative novelty of the issue of AI regulation, domestic and international evidence of successful approaches is still far from complete. However, from lessons learned through international collaboration and through the regulation of other technologies I am optimistic about the options available to governments and organisations across the world.

I am increasingly convinced that the international ethical and safe development and adoption of AI systems can be secured. It is my hope that governments, regulators, civil servants, and practitioners, whatever the jurisdiction, will accept the challenges and put these constructive proposals into practice.

With that hope comes my great thanks to my wife Jean for putting up with my AI preoccupation over the years, and to colleagues in politics, technology, professional life, and academia who have travelled on this journey with me over the past few years. Writing about AI has always involved the risk of aiming for a moving target and penning this book has been no exception. Particular thanks are due to Coran Darling who has contributed greatly by providing his own expertise and that of his professional colleagues. Any errors or oversimplifications, however, are entirely my own!

Tim Clement-Jones
January 2024

About the Author

Tim Clement-Jones

Tim Clement-Jones was Chair of the House of Lords Select Committee on Artificial Intelligence (2017–18) and is Co-Founder and Co-Chair of the All-Party Parliamentary Group on Artificial Intelligence. He was the initiator and a member of the recent House of Lords Select Committee inquiry into Autonomous Weapon Systems. He was made CBE for political services in 1988 and a life peer in 1998. He is now the Liberal Democrat spokesperson for Science Innovation and Technology in the House of Lords.

Until 2018 Tim was a Partner of the global law firm DLA Piper and its former London Managing Partner. He is now a consultant to the firm on AI policy and regulation. He is Chair of Trust Alliance Group (formerly Ombudsman Services Limited), the not-for-profit, independent ombudsman service that provides dispute resolution for communications and energy utilities, and Chair of the Council of Queen Mary University of London. He is a former consultant to the Council of Europe's AI Working Group (CAHAI) and is a member of the OECD's ONE AI Expert Group.

Assisted by Coran Darling

Coran Darling is an international technology practitioner in law, AI, and data analytics. His primary work revolves around helping organisations to navigate the challenges of technology, data, and life sciences. He is a member of the OECD's ONE AI Expert groups on AI risks and AI Incidents, a member of the Alan Turing Institute's Data Ethics Group, a founding committee member of the AI Group of the Society for Computers and Law, and a non-parliamentary member of the UK government's All-Party Parliamentary Groups for AI and Data Analytics. He is a Fellow of the Responsible AI Institute, a member of the European Commission's AI Alliance, a member of the US National Institute of Standards and Technology's working group on generative AI, contributor to the US Department of Commerce's AI Safety Consortium, and an advisor to the British Standards Institution on matters of artificial intelligence and data.

1 Introduction – The AI Narrative

Inescapably, for better or worse, as a society we are becoming increasingly conscious of the impact of artificial intelligence (AI) in its many forms. Barely a day goes by now without some reference to AI in the news, whether it is positive and relates to a new technology capable of making everyone's lives easier – or more negative – and warning of the systematic reduction of employment opportunities, as humans are replaced by automation. With the wide-scale adoption of digital and technological solutions over the past few years, especially as we attempted to minimise the impact of the COVID-19 pandemic, we have all become more aware of the importance of digital media and the impact that AI and algorithms have on our lives.

In December 2022, the United Kingdom's National AI Strategy[3] rightly identified AI as the 'fastest growing deep technology in the world, with huge potential to rewrite the rules of entire industries, drive substantial economic growth and transform all areas of life'. Wide-scale changes of this nature, brought about by the development of innovative technologies are, however, by no means a new experience. We need only look to previous industrial revolutions where major societal shifts occurred through the implementation of mechanical, electrical, and computing/automation assisted innovations. Benz began the first commercial production of motor vehicles with an internal combustion engine in 1886. By 1912, the number of vehicles in London exceeded the number of horses. What appears to have caught the world by surprise in the case of AI, with the potential it brings, is the speed and complexity with which it has arrived, forcing us to address many concerns that were previously concepts described in science fiction.

This rapid plunging of the world into a new technological frontier can be likened to the 1970s American television series, Soap. At the beginning of each episode, viewers would be introduced through a recap of the previous episode which would finish by exclaiming: 'Confused? You won't be, after this week's episode.' Shortly after, the plotline would continue to spiral into new unknowns and even more confusing stories.

This is certainly how it sometimes feels when tackling the narrative around AI as it swings back and forward between the extremes of a societal good with the potential to solve humanity's problems, such as climate change, to the opposite view, where AI is an existential threat to humanity and we should expect an imminent rise of the machines. This is unquestionably made worse by a general lack of public understanding of the technology and an increase in dramatic AI-related media headlines. An early and notable example was the lurid headline in response to the written by the UK's House of Lords Select Committee on AI which considered the economic, ethical, and social implications of advances in artificial intelligence. In response to our report in 2018 entitled *AI in the UK: Ready, willing and able?*, we were alarmingly warned:

'Killer Robots could become a reality unless a moral code is created for AI, peers warn.'[4]

Famously the late Professor Stephen Hawking warned that the creation of powerful artificial intelligence will be 'either the best, or the worst thing, ever to happen to humanity'.[5]

AI is not, however, despite what many headlines would lead us to believe, all doom and gloom. In reality, AI presents opportunities worldwide across a variety of sectors, such as healthcare, education, financial services, marketing, retail, agriculture, energy conservation, public services, smart or connected cities, and regulatory technology itself. The predictive, analytical, and problem-solving nature of AI, and in particular generative AI systems, has the potential to drastically improve performance, research outcomes, productivity, and customer experience.

A notable example of this is the marrying of biotechnology and AI-enabled data analytics in tackling the development of bespoke or 'precision' medicines. It has opened up the potential to synthesise, understand, and make use of far greater quantities of health information in the pursuit of treating diseases by creating novel therapies through newly identified compounds and precision medicines.

Regardless of which side of the fence one sits with respect to AI and its potential for benefit or harm, it is increasingly apparent that AI has already – and will to an even greater extent in future – become an integral part of everyday life. It brings many opportunities to overcome the challenges of the past, increasing diversity and access to employment for those who are presently unable to work through location or physical disabilities, and streamlining many administrative processes in business that are both costly and time-consuming.

We already have examples of its use in the detection of financial crimes, including fraudulent behaviour and anti-competitive practices, the delivery of personalised education and tutoring, energy conservation, medical care and treatment, and the delivery of large-scale government and non-governmental initiatives, including the United Nations' pursuit of their sustainable development goals, such as combating climate change, hunger, and poverty.

It is therefore of no surprise that many, including over a thousand technologists from the UK's Chartered Institute for Information Technology (BCS), asserted in an open letter in 2023 that AI will be a transformative force for good if the right critical decisions about its development and use are made.[6]

It is equally apparent, however, that AI has the potential for a great many harms to individuals, their rights, and society as a whole. This was recognised directly in March 2023 in a letter signed by several thousand technologists, including those from academia, government, and technology companies themselves, recognising 'profound risks to society and humanity' posed by AI and systems with human-competitive intelligence and calling for a temporary halt on technological developments while risks were assessed.[7]

Later in May of the same year another group of technologists led by the Center for AI Safety, including Dr Geoff Hinton, one of the godfathers of deep neural networks, and several senior leaders behind many of the AI technologies that we see on the market today asserted in a short, concerned statement that 'mitigating the risk of extinction from AI should be a global priority alongside other societal-scale risks such as pandemics and nuclear war'. Unsurprisingly, given such existential concerns, Dr Hinton subsequently resigned from his previously held role at Google to 'speak freely about the dangers of AI'.[8]

Many of those seeking to draw attention to the potential risks of AI do not, however, accept that moratoriums or bans should be put in place as if AI – in particular generative AI – were a form of inhumane technology. Instead, many, including a number of prominent tech executives, believe that a controlled approach should be taken that involves comprehensive regulation with a specific international agency created for the oversight and monitoring of AI developments.

Sam Altman the CEO of OpenAI for example, in giving evidence to the US Congress, rejected the idea of a temporary moratorium on AI development but asked for AI to be regulated. He cited existential risk, and espoused an international agency along the lines of the International Atomic Energy Agency (IAEA) being created to oversee AI development and its risks.[9]

As a cautious optimist, the author believes that new technology has the potential to offer a great many benefits, including greater productivity and more efficient use of resources. But as highlighted in the title of Stephanie Hare's book, *Technology is Not Neutral*,[10] we should be clear about the purpose of new technology when we adopt it and about the way in which we intend to adopt it. We need to ask a number of questions: Even if AI can do something, should it? Does it better connect and empower our citizens and improve working life? Does it create a more sustainable society?

A cardinal principle in the development of effective governance of AI should be the requirement that some sort of societal (or organisational) good must come from the implementation of technology. In short, deployment of AI should be guided in such a way that its central purpose is to promote individual or societal benefit, rather than be implemented in a push for automation as an end in itself.

The author's view is that, as part of the process of adoption, a governance framework should be developed and implemented in a way that encourages transparency and is designed to gain and develop stakeholder trust. The author also believes that we must seek to actively shape AI's development and utilisation across all stages of its lifecycle – including decommissioning – or risk passively acquiescing to its many predictable consequences.

Even where a clear purpose and benefit are identified, ineffective governance has the potential to cause further concerns. Anyone who has read *Weapons of Math Destruction* by Cathy O'Neil or Hannah Fry's *Hello World: How to be Human in the Age of the Machine*[11,12] will be only too aware of the impact of algorithms on our lives already and of their implications for vulnerable and disadvantaged individuals and communities.

Ensuring freedom from unintended bias in AI systems and avoiding discriminatory decisions and outputs in relation to particular genders, ages, and ethnicities is essential. Failure to do so risks the discriminatory practices becoming embedded in the deployment of an algorithm and of exacerbating many of the issues they are designed to resolve. For example, concern has arisen in the United States over bias displayed in algorithms responsible for predictive policing and the administration of criminal justice, such as COMPAS,[13] a tool used by US courts to assess the likelihood of a defendant becoming a recidivist.

As is explored later, progress (and indeed attitudes towards the desired shape of governance) still varies considerably between governments across the world. The UK government, unlike the EU, is unconvinced by the need to regulate at this juncture and has mainly focused on existential risk, and its proposed approach to regulatory intervention reflects this.

At the time of writing, the EU has elected to take a different route and in December 2023 agreed to a position on their proposed EU Regulation – the 'AI Act' – mandating a comprehensive risk-based framework for legislating AI in the market.[14] The US has, to date, opted for a hybrid of the two approaches by implementing an Executive Order on the Safe, Secure, and Trustworthy use of AI in the US[15] that (among other requirements) mandates obligations to existing federal departments, agencies, and regulators for further action on their part and also through the bipartisan introduction of several AI-specific bills into Congress, such as the Artificial Intelligence Research, Innovation, and Accountability Act of 2023 which could well create a similar set of risk-based protocols for regulation of AI systems.

In spite of the many differing approaches, it does appear that an element of conformity is emerging on international goals for AI governance. In October 2023, shortly after a meeting of digital and tech ministers,[16] G7 governments issued a statement on what is called 'the Hiroshima AI process'[17] declaring both:

We, the Leaders of the Group of Seven (G7), stress the innovative opportunities and transformative potential of advanced Artificial Intelligence (AI) systems, in particular, foundation models and generative AI.

And

We also recognize the need to manage risks and to protect individuals, society, and our shared principles including the rule of law and democratic values, keeping humankind at the center.

It proceeded to endorse a set of Hiroshima Process International Guiding Principles and Code of Conduct for Organizations Developing Advanced AI Systems and 'instructed acceleration' of cooperation with and between the Global Partnership on Artificial Intelligence (GPAI) and the Organisation for Economic Co-operation and Development (OECD),[18] the former aiming to function as a non-exhaustive set of principles that organisations and governments should consider in the promotion of safe, secure, and trustworthy AI. We outline these later.

The following month the UK held an International AI Safety Summit at Bletchley Park, itself closely connected with one of the founders of AI, Alan Turing, which at its conclusion delivered the so-called Bletchley Declaration, signed by 28 countries plus the EU.[19]

In essence, the Declaration set out an agenda for future cooperation between countries in the international governance of AI, which included identifying and understanding AI safety risks of shared concern and building risk-based policies to ensure international safety in light of these risks.

Whatever one's views about the effectiveness of statements such as this there is no doubt that increased international collaboration in tackling AI is needed if an effective means of governing the technology at an organisational, national, and international level needs to be developed.

While the phrase 'existential risk' is in our view overly dramatic, my motive for writing this book is nevertheless a shared sense of urgency. AI – and indeed technology as a whole – brings with it challenges and risks that have the potential to impact the rights and safety of individuals and organisations across the world. Failure to recognise them poses a threat to the retention of public trust in AI and will undermine much of the work of innovators in demonstrating the many potential benefits of new developments in technology.

As governments and legislators face the challenge of regulating new and developing technologies, some comfort can be taken from the fact that myths, parables, and fiction have prepared us for the impact of the interaction of humans and new technology. We have the example of King Midas of the ancient Greek myth, who much like a naive programmer of today, was too literal in his request, so that everything he touched, his daughter included, turned to gold.

Perhaps we have been prepared by another ancient story, that of Talos the bronze humanoid colossus, reputedly forged by the god Hephaestus, the god of invention and blacksmithing, to protect the island of Crete against invaders. He was encountered by Jason and the Argonauts on their return from stealing the Golden Fleece.[20]

A classic demonstration that what technology produces, even in complete compliance with commands, may be completely contrary to our actual intentions. More recently in the 20th century Isaac Asimov's *I, Robot* stories[21] showed us that even when we think we have prepared for multiple outcomes and set rules, technology can deliver unintended consequences.

Despite these narratives, it remains difficult for us to easily frame or fully understand the extent of the threats and opportunities presented by new technologies, such as foundation AI models, general-purpose AI, and biometric data recognition, in particular, where they differ from their less sophisticated predecessors. For example, should we make a distinction between AI used as an initial customer service chatbot and its use in a complex large language model or generative AI program such as those powered by GPT models? If so, how do we actually go about doing that?

The challenges posed by the sheer volume of emerging technologies and novel applications of AI is only matched by their complexity in design and function. Where once we dealt with regulation of rudimentary computational devices and its software, we now have to consider the implications of quantum computers, able to vastly outperform their predecessors and perform previously inconceivable tasks. Although we have not yet reached the stage of Artificial General Intelligence (AGI), the potential and perceived creativity of AI continues to grow.

In October 2022, for example, legislators – and the rest of the world – watched as, while sitting beside its human creator, the robot artist Ai-Da appeared before the UK House of Lords to give evidence on the subject of AI, robotics, and the creative arts.[22] More recently the large language models GPT-4, Claude, and Bard have demonstrated their abilities as authors. Multimodal AI systems that combine a range of capabilities, language, image recognition and data analysis and that give every appearance of AGI are in active development.

The emergence of these technologies and intelligent systems and the challenges they bring means that, much like Sisyphus eternally pushing up his unrelenting boulder, legislators and regulators have the unenviable job of responding to the continuous pressure of rapidly evolving technology.

Owing to this newfound complexity and superfast evolution, the ability of legislators and regulators to catch up with defining the AI technologies they seek to regulate – as well as responding to the risks posed and opportunities they offer to society – is becoming increasingly difficult. Even more difficult, once they have these parameters pinned down, is the decision as to what extent and through what means we actually go about regulation.

Technology is now at the point where a 'deploy-and-forget' approach is no longer viable. As it learns in operation and becomes increasingly autonomous it opens its own form of technology Pandora's box. This is well illustrated by Brian Christian in *The Alignment Problem and* Professor Stuart Russell in *Human Compatible*.[23] Each, in their expert ways, warns of the risks in treating AI in the same way as other forms of software and computer programs. Professor Russell, in particular, prescribes building uncertainty into the delivery of objectives of AI systems so that having a human in the loop is not just desirable but necessary as part of effective governance.

Both advocate a form of governance and regulation of AI systems that ensures that potential risks to humanity are mitigated through embedding specific standards which ensure that the AI needs meaningful human input to fully define and accomplish its objectives.

In order to build the foundation for a successful method of regulation, many questions need to be answered along the way, including:

- Is substitution or augmentation of human potential by machines always ethically or societally appropriate? Should there be an obligation to reserve certain roles specifically for humans or keep a human in the loop, even where technology can provide faster, higher quality, and more cost-efficient results?
- How should we (indeed, can we) regulate AI systems that actively impersonate human characteristics and replicate individual human identities?
- What is the most appropriate way of regulating a moving target like AI? Are there risks that are uniform throughout the various classes of AI and technology that can be anticipated, and can they be mitigated at their source by, for instance, common standards of risk assessment?
- Do international standards offer a solution for areas where domestic regulation falls short? Is reaching agreement on common standards practically possible?

It is the intention of this book to seek to address these questions, and others, in the chapters that follow.

It should be stated at the outset that talk of innovation-friendly regulation is not always helpful and often has the potential to direct regulators down a path that, while well intended, does not accurately achieve the kind of effective governance that they are seeking to implement. Effective and well-tailored regulation, in our view, is about assessing and calibrating risk and providing the necessary guardrails for high-impact outcomes. Innovation is only one of these many outcomes. It can be either desirable or undesirable and is not always an unqualified benefit and certainly should not be the only focus for the legislator or regulator.

Our central theme throughout is that we must find ways, ahead of the development of AGI, of ensuring that AI in its current and future form, for the sake of the future of humanity, is our servant not our master. That, here and now, is the challenging and urgent task for policymakers that forms the essence of this book.

The author intends this book to have relevance and applicability across many jurisdictions. While its focus lies primarily within the United Kingdom, insights and developments are drawn from other jurisdictions, including the United States, the European Union, and beyond.

It initially sets out the principal risks encountered during the implementation of AI and AI-powered technology. The remainder of the chapters set out the various challenges that follow interaction between human and machine in different common contexts, the ways in which they can be tackled, and the current approaches taken by the jurisdictions that are, at the time of writing, currently leading the charge in the governance and regulation of AI.

The author has some faith that by regulating for the risks, developing the necessary skills, and cooperating internationally we can succeed in harnessing these technologies for optimum human benefit, but it is by no means a foregone conclusion.

2 AI Risks: What Are They and How Do We Assess Them?

A common goal for effective governance of AI to date in the early development of AI governance and regulatory frameworks has been the encouragement of innovation while identifying and mitigating areas of risk.

This chapter seeks to set the scene for this goal by identifying AI risks, how they can be classified and, subsequently, how they can appropriately be addressed through well-considered governance frameworks.

Risk identification and assessment

The manner in which risks are identified and planned for are, it seems, heavily influenced by the political benefits that governments and organisations seek to derive from addressing them. Governments, for example, are likely to be restricted by the timing of election cycles and therefore seek to address risks that can be seen within a typical election cycle – often four or five years. In democratic countries, because they typically have short electoral cycles, there are both cultural and institutional flaws in planning, assessment mitigation, and proactive prevention. The time is never ripe for expenditure on risk prevention and mitigation.

Where there is longer tenure, or outlook, such as those running regulators or agencies or on the boards of organisations, they may have longer timeframes to work with and therefore may look further ahead in their approach to identifying and planning for risks.

Institutions that are seeking to prepare for those risks that are identified (however distant or unlikely) must also consider the overall cost–benefit of acting on potential risks. For example, it is far more likely that a government in a country where water is a scarce resource will benefit from early resource planning and development of regulatory powers that allow for tighter controls on use of water than a government which governs a country with a much lower chance of suffering from droughts and extreme weather events. In similar fashion, it is much more prudent and beneficial for a government with advanced deployment of technology to implement measures to ensure its effective and safe use than a country with less prolific use of technology.

The governance of technology presents particular challenges in terms of the approach to identification of risks and subsequent planning. Professor Lord Martin Rees, Co-Founder of the Cambridge Centre for the Study of Existential Risk, identifies the governance balancing act that is required by many political institutions and organisations to play with this type of risk identification and planning in his book *On the Future: Prospects for Humanity*.

> *Politicians have incentives to prepare for localized floods, terrorist acts, and other hazards that are more likely to materialise within a given political cycle. But they have less incentive to prepare for events that are unfamiliar and global—even for high consequence/low probability events that are so devastating that one occurrence is too many.*[24]

Whatever justification is given for shorter-term planning across recent government interventions, it is clear that the approach of governments to identification and planning of critical risks has rarely prioritised problems beyond high-visibility short-term risks. In the case of the US, priorities are often associated with what can be easily shown within a presidential or congressional term, which can then be used in a campaign for re-election or to directly attack the policies of their opponent.

Similar short-term risk identification and planning is equally present in the UK. The 2021 House of Lords Special *Inquiry into Risk Assessment and Risk Planning*,[25] concluded that the UK national risk assessment system is heavily deficient in assessing and planning for chronic or long-term risks, and has a bias against low-likelihood, high-impact risks. Perhaps more concerning was the UK government's inability to address harms caused by rapidly changing and developing technologies, it was discovered that even medium-term risks were often ill-accounted-for without even considering more generational changes such as climate change, pandemics, and large-scale changes to the economy as a result of automation. This view was bluntly summarised by Sir Patrick Vallance, the UK government's former

Chief Scientific Adviser in his evidence to the Committee, as 'If you take a two-year outlook, you get the wrong answer.'[26]

Paradoxically at the opposite end of the spectrum, there have been advocates justifying short-term thinking. During the taking of oral evidence at a meeting of the Select Committee the then Director of the Cabinet Office's Civil Contingencies Secretariat (CCS) – which supports the Civil Contingencies Committee, known as COBRA – claimed that:

> the shorter the timeframe, the more nuanced a story we can construct about the risk. On longer timeframes, we have a greater degree of uncertainty about the direction the risk takes. This is an important factor, because ultimately the purpose of this is not to make the best possible articulation of what the risk might be; the purpose is to aid planning. Therefore, that greater specificity has benefits for organisations as they are choosing what to focus their planning on.[27]

The shortcomings of this approach, however, became apparent in the international response by governments to the COVID-19 pandemic in which failure to adequately plan for a major pandemic led to a scrambled, ill-fated attempt to prevent the spread of the virus. This was well illustrated in the report by the Institute for Government report in 2022 *Managing Extreme Risks*,[28] which dispelled any idea that the UK government was well prepared and able to identify and mitigate existential risks beyond those that could be actively addressed in the short term.

There is no doubt, however, that the risks we face are changing, and new risks continue to emerge in ways that were previously relegated to the realms of science fiction. Technological advances have raised the threat posed by the malicious deployment of technologies, which could be used for good or ill, and the ability for control of essential elements of infrastructure to be impacted by malicious action.

At the beginning of his book on government approach to risk planning, *Apocalypse How?*[29] former UK Cabinet Minister Sir Oliver Letwin posits a national emergency in which the internet goes down, electricity supply fails across the country without any contingency put in place and there is no analogue telephone backup available. The failure of critical infrastructure is not a fanciful scenario as the experience of Ukraine in 2023 demonstrates, where it was alleged that satellite communications infrastructure was taken offline, rendering drones deployed during the course of battle which relied on them for navigation completely ineffective.[30]

While it is perhaps a less likely consequence of the deployment of AI, failure to appropriately identify risks and appropriate contingency measures at an early stage undoubtedly could lead to a major future societal crisis.

Former political journalist, now author, Robert Harris giving evidence during the UK *House of Lords Inquiry into Risk Assessment and Risk Planning*, asserted: 'Sophisticated societies do collapse. Every civilisation collapses. You cannot think of one that did not face some terrible crisis, partly because they became so sophisticated.'[31]

In response to many of the lessons learned over the past few years, however, governments have been taking positive, albeit slow, steps towards better planning for risks, technological or otherwise. The UK, for example, has since amended its policy approach to risk to account for risks that fall within a five-year timeframe. However, it is unclear how these medium-term approaches can address the risks that are associated with technology and the ongoing development of AI.

Chronic risks such as large-scale unemployment, chronologically unpredictable risks such as the impacts of artificial general intelligence, low-likelihood risks such as complete shutdown of digital infrastructure, and the most significant (albeit minimally likely) risks such as direct conflict between humans and machines need to be accompanied by a long-term assessment, which should, in the author's view, be of the order of at least 15 years. After all, that is the minimum period which is expected even for local development plans.[32] There is a danger that the current timeframe adopted by most Western democracies for assessing likelihood and impact will lead to misplaced confidence, particularly in terms of the risks posed by new technology – a similar confidence that these democracies had when going into the initial throes of the COVID-19 pandemic.

When it comes to the identification of risks posed by AI and related technologies, several options are available to those charged with the task. There are, for example, many attractions to the classification system of

Professor Ortwin Renn of Stuttgart University,[33] through which risks are classified based on how they need to be managed. He uses a range of indicators to provide a more in-depth representation of the risk, including: extent of damage, probability of occurrence, uncertainty, ubiquity, persistence, reversibility, delayed effect between event and impact, what he calls 'violation of equity', and potential for social disorder.

Professor Renn's system suggests that these risks should be treated differently, both in evaluation of their impact and in management strategies. He distils these criteria into six risk classes, and assigns them names from Greek mythology:

- **Damocles' sword**: high-impact, low-probability risks such as technological risks from nuclear energy and large-scale chemical facilities.

- **Cyclops**: high-impact risks with significant uncertainty in the likelihood assessment, natural events, such as floods and earthquakes.

- **Pythia**: risks where the extent of impact, the size of impact, and the likelihood are highly uncertain, e.g. human interventions in ecosystems.

- **Pandora's box**: risks where there is uncertainty in both impact and likelihood, and the damage would be irreversible, persistent, and wide-ranging, e.g. the use of organic pollutants and the impact of some AI systems.

- **Cassandra**: risks where the likelihood and impact are both high and relatively well-known but there is delay between the triggering event and the occurrence of damage, leading to low societal concern, e.g. anthropogenic climate change and, it could be argued, artificial general intelligence.

- **Medusa**: low probability and low damage risks where there is a large gap between public risk perception and expert risk analysis, e.g. mobile phone usage and electromagnetic fields.

Whatever system of identification and assessment is employed it must clearly be implemented in such a way that allows governments and organisations to account for risks that are not only easy to resolve within a short period of time, but that may pose greater, albeit remote, risks to society.

AI and its risks

In order to adequately plan and prepare for the risks of AI, it is necessary to understand exactly what is meant by the term. On this there has been no consensus. Definitions range from sets of techniques aimed at approximating aspects of human or animal cognition using machines (Ryan Calo, *Artificial Intelligence Policy: A Primer and Roadmap*[34]) to the ability of computer systems to solve problems and to perform tasks that typically require human intelligence (*The Final Report of the National Security Commission on AI in the US*[35]).

A common definition, which has been recommended by the International Organization for Standardization (ISO) and others, is:

> *[An i]nterdisciplinary field, usually regarded as a branch of computer science, dealing with models and systems for the performance of functions generally associated with human intelligence, such as reasoning and learning.*[36]

Then we have the practical definition of AI developed by Brad Smith and Carol Ann Browne in their book *Tools and Weapons: The Promise and the Peril of the Digital Age* is 'software that learns from experience'[37] – which is wide enough to capture current incarnations of the technology, while accounting for future developments that cannot currently be accounted for.

While helpful in understanding the concept and practice behind AI, the proliferation of definitions has undoubtedly created some confusion. Recent government proposals, including the European Union's (EU) AI Regulatory framework and the US Executive Order on Safe, Secure, and Trustworthy AI have, however, now adopted the OECD's revised definition from November 2023 which provides some international consistency:

> *a machine-based system that, for explicit or implicit objectives, infers,*

from the input it receives, how to generate outputs such as predictions, content, recommendations, or decisions that can influence physical or virtual environments. Different AI systems vary in their levels of autonomy and adaptiveness after deployment.[38]

The definition reflects developments in AI over several years, including advances in generative AI capabilities, and will in our view continue to serve as the foundation for regulatory and legislative intervention internationally.

Even if they are not yet AGI, or able to compete in every sphere with humans, AI neural networks or algorithms are far more sophisticated than ordinary computer programs – generating outputs, decisions, and predictions on the basis of machine learning, based on vast quantities of data, sophisticated semiconductors, and enormous computing power.

AI has moved on from systems being able to play chess and GO, to being able to beat veteran players at the game Diplomacy, where victories are determined by negotiation and prediction of human responses to propositions, in order to convince other players to act in favour. While it is accepted that the AI does not embody the emotion and empathy with which human decisions are made, it is clear that they are rapidly developing convincing capabilities that 'read' and mirror them.

AI is already having a major impact on our lives, and many countries are setting comprehensive strategies to harness it. The anticipated economic benefits over this decade are significant, with estimates predicting that AI will bring an additional $900 billion in global revenue by 2026 (*Bank of America Global Research*).[39] Across the world COVID-19 has emphasised and accelerated the dependence of virtually every business and sector on the successful adoption of the latest relevant technologies for their survival.

What is clear is that AI is not a conventional technological advance. Many AI systems have a high degree not only of computational intelligence but also of autonomy, which marks them out for public concern. The degree of autonomy, lack of human intervention or control, and the black box nature of some systems makes it an entirely different proposition compared to other technology that we have previously had the challenge of seeking to govern and regulate.

Mustafa Suleyman in his book *The Coming Wave*[40] says that the risk issues around AI are all about the future in terms of preparing for the consequences of AGI, but there are real current risks here and now which need tackling.

When asked what comes to mind when considering the risks of AI, the risk of bias – that is the instance of an AI producing results that are systematically prejudicial towards certain outcomes based on erroneous assumptions, training, inputs, or data – is often cited as a primary concern. It is understandable that this is the case. The risk of being unfairly impacted by the decisions or outputs of an AI or AI-powered system will lead many to scepticism and mistrust if they are unfairly based on characteristics such as gender or race, or the denial of credit. While there are certain practical measures that can be taken, such as careful curation of the data used, it is nonetheless a real concern that requires a level of governance that ensures fairness throughout the application of the technology.

The ability to generate misinformation is equally a prominent concern and a major risk of the deployment of AI. An early example arose in June 2023, when two lawyers in reliance on the information provided to them by ChatGPT inadvertently included cases in court filings that, while appearing to be convincing precedents, were completely fabricated.[41] Often referred to as 'hallucinations', these instances of false information highlight the limitations of many AI programs, particularly large language models, and emphasise the need for minimum standards of accuracy, minimum levels of output supervision, and sufficient training for those interacting with AI to understand that they will not always produce truthful and accurate information.

Of even greater concern is its ability to create disinformation – the purposeful dissemination of false information created with the intent to harm individuals or groups. The concern is of such magnitude that intelligence agencies across the world have publicly acknowledged and warned of the potential for AI to be used as a tool in the delivery of false information, in the performance of scams, and in the direct interference in democratic processes. Many of these specific risks are detailed further in Chapter 3 in a discussion of the threats to democracy, human rights, and the rule of law posed by the operation of AI systems.

The right to privacy and the risk of invasive practices are also a recurring theme in the discussion of concerns surrounding AI. This may stem from the ability to process and analyse much larger amounts of personal data relating to an individual which can then be used in the provision of services such as healthcare, insurance, and advertisements through to more direct intervention such as active surveillance through live facial recognition technology, particularly in public areas.

In the UK, despite the efforts of Parliamentarians and organisations such as the Ada Lovelace Institute and Big Brother Watch, there is no recognition by the UK government that explicit legislation and/or regulation for intrusive AI technology such as live facial recognition is needed to prevent the arrival of the surveillance state. Comparatively, in the EU and in several cities across the US, indiscriminate use of facial recognition surveillance has been banned.

There is understandable concern about the potentially significant impact of AI on jobs and the workplace. The forecasts of the displacement of human jobs by automation vary widely but there is no doubt that many traditional jobs are already being displaced. The author does not believe that the adoption of AI is making – or will necessarily make – huge numbers of people redundant in the short term, but the nature of work will undoubtedly change, and a concerted programme of adjustment and retraining for different jobs and skills will be required. This is discussed in Chapter 6.

On the defence front, as also discussed in more detail later, new technologies are changing how military operations are conducted. Autonomous drone warfare is already a fact of life. The UN Secretary General, António Guterres has previously stated, 'Autonomous machines with the power and discretion to select targets and take lives without human involvement are politically unacceptable, morally repugnant and should be prohibited by international law.'[42] In spite of this, no concrete international agreement on the prohibition or limitation of such weapons has been made and there is equally no guarantee that this will be adhered to in battlefields where the technological upper hand is a deciding factor. Equally, in a manner similar to the development of weapons during the runup to the Second World War and the Cold War, rapid increases in research and development of these weapons may create a new technological arms race, where development of AI and the control of AI is an ongoing battle.

In a not-so-dissimilar fashion, organisations may equally find themselves in a race for control and dominance of AI and the resources on which they rely – including data, computational power ('compute'), and infrastructure. Often described as the 'Winners Take All Risk', there is a real risk, particularly as a result of what are called network effects, that those with the ability to rapidly be first to market will continue to grow their overall share of the market to the point where nearly all AI resources could be held in the hands of a very select few organisations. Search services, communication technologies, and the provision of cloud services where much of the market is concentrated with a few dominant market players are already examples of this.

Again these aspects are discussed in more detail in later chapters.

Overdependence on AI has also been cited by Professor Lord Rees[43] as a key risk which anticipates even greater reliance than we are already placing on AI functions. In interacting with AI, harms may well arise from users overly trusting them, or treating them as if they were human. A relatively benign example is the decline in map reading skills post Google Maps and other navigation applications. Far more concerning is the example of the Horizon computer software, relied on, against all the evidence to the contrary, by Post Office staff as they took sub-postmasters to court. Hence the imperative to reform the Computer Misuse Act 1990 to enable legitimate independent testing of computer systems and the reform of court rules of evidence which make the presumption that computer evidence is accurate unless proven otherwise.[44]

This risk could become far more critical as the AI capabilities we rely on become greater. This is particularly likely to be the case given human tendency to anthropomorphise, or ascribe human qualities to AI and robots, which in turn occasionally leads to misplaced trust.

The peculiarities of frontier AI

New developments in AI systems, so-called frontier AI technologies such as ChatGPT and other large language models, have in turn required definition to pin them down for governance and regulatory purposes. To date, several approaches have been taken by governments across the world, including the UK and the EU. In the case of the UK, while it was acknowledged that the definition is likely to develop, a recent discussion paper by the Government Office for Science (GOS)[45] settled on:

> *highly capable general-purpose AI models that can perform a wide variety of tasks and match or exceed the capabilities present in today's most advanced models.*

The discussion paper noted that while large language models form the primary example at present, multimodal models (such as those that also include generation of images, sound, and video) are also increasingly common, and this space is likely to develop as more advanced AI models emerge.

This definition has the merit of being sufficiently wide to capture several of the large language and multimodal models we see on the market today, as well as leave an element of flexibility for future developments not currently considered, but it does nothing to describe the underlying technology.

The European Parliament's definition of foundation models in their own regulatory proposal leading into the final discussions with Council and Commission in the autumn of 2023 was more comprehensive, going beyond their capabilities and instead focusing on their composition and purpose:

> *AI system models trained on large and diverse datasets, designed for generality of output that can be used for many different tasks.*[46]

Precise definition may be elusive, but it can be said that these types of AI systems are broadly developed in two main stages: pre-training prior to deployment and fine-tuning once up and running.

In the pre-training phase, frontier AI systems devour substantial quantities of text, documents, and other content. The system begins to learn by predicting the subsequent word in a text, originally one word at a time, then in sentences. Initially, its predictions are quite random, but as it goes through more data, it learns from its errors and enhances its predictive accuracy. After the pre-training phase, the model becomes exceptionally good, even surpassing human abilities on occasion, in predicting the next word or whole sentence in a randomly selected document.

After this the so-called agentification stage uses reinforcement learning with human feedback to transform the model from a passive generator of outputs into an active agent that can interact with its environment. Agentification marks the transition from a static generative model to an interactive agent capable of learning from its environment and responding to it in a dynamic and adaptive manner.

Once the fine-tuning stage is reached, the large language model (LLM) continues training, using carefully curated datasets. These datasets are designed for more specific tasks or are used to guide the model's behaviour in line with the expected values and abilities assigned to the model.

As the definitions demonstrate, frontier AI systems are typically designed to perform a wide variety of tasks, whether this be to augment capabilities of those seeking to use the technology or to completely replace them in certain aspects of work.

These include:

- Conversing fluently and at length, drawing on extensive information contained in training data, which may be used for use cases such as chatbots.
- Writing long sequences of well-functioning code from natural language instructions, including making new apps, thereby speeding up development processes.
- Generating new content and assisting in the dissemination of information by news outlets.
- Translating language.
- Accelerating academic research.

Where frontier AI has the potential to truly excel is in augmenting existing tools. A common example of this is the enhancement of existing documentation software (such as Word) with the purpose of providing inspiration, changing tone of writing, and quickly summarising large quantities of information for the purposes of expanding existing and creating further chapters within the same context.

What is becoming increasingly apparent is that the potential for frontier AI may be even greater than we have been able to determine to date. The technology industry itself – indeed every other industry – continues to learn as the technology is developed and explored. It is expected that with enhancements such as better prompts and tools in the hands of the user, better structures for information flow, the ability to fine-tune data inputted, and the ability to link multiple AI systems, new capabilities will begin to emerge, thereby revolutionising further aspects of the work we do.

However, despite the great – and in many ways unknown – potential of these systems, it has become very clear that frontier AI, and generative AI and LLMs in particular, have their own additional risks and challenges. If the model does not meet the requirements of the proposed task, it will be inherently limited and unable to perform as intended. These limitations, as the GOS discussion paper highlights, may lead to instances of inaccuracy and hallucinations, and an inability to maintain context and coherence over extended interactions and use.

Researchers at DeepMind have identified six broad categories of risk:

- Discrimination, hate speech and exclusion arising from model outputs producing discriminatory and exclusionary content.
- Information hazards whereby the dissemination of private or sensitive information can cause harm.
- Misinformation harms arising from model outputs producing false or misleading information.
- Malicious uses arising from actors using foundation models to intentionally cause harm.
- Human-computer interaction harms arising from users overly trusting the foundation model, or treating them as if they are human.
- Automation, access and environmental harms arising from the environmental or downstream economic impacts of the foundation model.[47]

Before the Bletchley AI Safety Summit, the head of the UK's then Foundation Model Taskforce – now the AI Safety Institute – was quoted as saying that he worried that our ability to create advanced systems would outpace our ability to manage the risks and that our current lack of understanding in the face of the challenge, he said, was 'quite striking'.[48]

Alongside technical risks and considerations, safety risk is another feature of frontier AI. For example, use of open-domains and a reliance on external resources, including open-source code and publicly sourced data often make models much more susceptible to security risks, reducing the technical robustness of a tool developed in this manner.

Once past the stage of design and development, testing of the safety of frontier models is an equally challenging element. At present, there is no common clear minimum safety standard or best practice to adhere to.

An additional feature is the potential for certain systems to develop patterns of behaviour that may even make monitoring their compliance with these standards beyond the capabilities of humans, adding an additional layer to safety concerns.

Beyond these safety concerns is the potential of frontier AI, particularly generative AI, to influence society and political activities. The ability of these systems to near flawlessly imitate or create copies of images and video, speech, and text creates a new vector of attack through synthetic media otherwise known as deepfakes, which can already be created by downloading an app on a mobile phone.

A political figure can be realistically impersonated and synthesised reciting wholly fictitious content. It can easily be imagined how this could be utilised to influence political processes during election times through swaying unsuspecting voters. There is also growing evidence of widespread use of deepfake technology in creating realistic pornographic images and videos using both celebrities and children without consent. Beyond this, use of these systems makes it much easier to create online discourse at speed. Bad actors can simply input a prompt that can then be used to distribute misinformation at scale within society, such as on vaccine side effects or about particular celebrities.

So frontier AI and its easy access capabilities very much form a double-edged sword. It can be used for good, but also for harm. Generative AI, if not properly trained with restrictions or rules to prevent the dissemination of certain information, may be used by bad actors for obtaining otherwise difficult-to-find information. A notable example of this is the manipulation of generative AI systems by non-state actors in the pursuit of information relating to the creation of home-made weaponry, including chemical weapons and explosives. Failure to systematically develop safeguards will leave opportunities for such actors to obtain information that they would not otherwise be able to, with potentially catastrophic consequences.

Furthermore, the Centre for the Governance of AI[49] has outlined how open-sourcing these AI models could amplify these risks, in particular of malicious use. They say models may become safe to open-source in the future as 'societal resilience to AI risk increases and improved safety mechanisms are developed'. They advocate government regulation and alternatives to open-sourcing, including gradual or 'staged' model release, model access for researchers and auditors, and clear industry standards based on an understanding of the risks posed by releasing model components.

Next steps

The risks outlined in this chapter arising from AI systems, including frontier AI models, are not necessarily a reason for their development to be restricted or prohibited. Preparing for them, however, does mean taking a much longer timescale into consideration and changing both our public and private risk assessment and risk planning mechanisms accordingly. But even if we have the right risk planning and assessment in place for these substantial AI risks the question remains how can we mitigate them?

As described in subsequent chapters, we need to ensure that the benefits of AI can be protected through governance frameworks and internal safety mechanisms which ensure the adoption of ethical and safety standards. There is an important role for corporate governance in this respect, as we will explore later. However, it is clearly a role that cannot be simply left to developers and adopters. Just as governments need to assess and plan for risk, they also need to legislate and regulate to mitigate risk. How to go about this in respect of AI systems is the subject of future chapters.

3 Digital Dividend or Deficit? Threats to Democracy and Freedom of Speech

In the previous chapter, some of the risks posed by various types of AI systems, in particular, generative AI models, were laid out. Many of these have the potential to significantly impact the established functioning of societies, particularly those characterised as democratic. As societies begin to grapple with many of these challenges, it becomes crucial to go beyond the headlines and take a look at the extent to which AI has the potential to impact many of the rights and freedoms within society that we take for granted.

AI, disinformation and the threat to democracy

Earlier in the book, attention was drawn to an open letter of March 2023 which called for a temporary moratorium on the development and training of powerful generative AI systems. One of the concerns raised was their potential ability to significantly impact the current functioning of society, whether through overt rapid and fundamental societal change or in a more subtle form through the dissemination of targeted disinformation. At the time of writing, over 30,000 signatories have joined in support.

The letter raises a number of important questions in the context of democracy, human rights, and the rule of law, such as:

> *should we let machines flood our information channels with propaganda and untruth?*[50]

While the author does not share their prescription – a moratorium on AI development – it is the case that AI raises a number of fundamental issues that have the potential to impact key features of democracy such as open debate, human rights, and free speech, and other fundamental rights ostensibly afforded to citizens by constitutional protections such as the

US Constitution, the European Convention on Human Rights, the UK Human Rights Act, or the UN Universal Declaration of Human Rights.

This is not the first time that concerns about the impact of new technologies and their capabilities on democracy, human rights, and the rule of law have been raised. Take the internet. In 2019, Senior Correspondent for VOX, Dylan Matthews observed that 'The internet was supposed to save democracy'.[51]

He continues:

> *The web, and in particular social media platforms like Facebook and Twitter, were supposed to make information easier and freer to share, to advantage the citizen at the expense of governments, to provide access to more information and viewpoints and more vibrant debates than residents of democracies had ever experienced before. It was supposed to topple dictators, to build social collaboration, to punish defection and isolation. Now, in 2018, the familiar techno-utopian pronouncements of the 1990s and '00s seem not just wrong but like a bad joke. … How could we have gotten this so wrong?*

These disillusioned comments came in response to several major technological abuses at the time, going to the very heart of the democratic process, including alleged instances of voter manipulation by pro-Russian/state-sanctioned groups during the 2016 US Presidential Election and the psychographic profiling of social media users by the then Cambridge Analytica,[52] leading up to the UK's vote on whether to leave the EU. This involved using data scraped online from millions of personal Facebook accounts to create personality profiles for voters and to target them with specific misinformation.

In each instance, misinformation and disinformation was targeted at unsuspecting social media users as a means of swaying their opinion and therefore changing their voting preference. It has been said, though this has not been, and is unlikely to be, confirmed by any conclusive evidence, that interference of this type contributed to the outcomes of both these democratic votes, suggesting the direct capability of technology to influence democracy, speech, and many of our individual rights.

In the intervening years since the Cambridge Analytica scandal, with the advent of AI-generated and amplified viral disinformation on social media these issues become even starker. The rapid development in the capabilities of AI, particularly when added to existing technologies, such as search engines and social media platforms, has the potential to amplify these impacts to a much greater scale and level of severity. This is made worse due to our relative lack of understanding of the sheer scale at which the operation of AI is already impacting us.

During a keynote address at Stanford University in April 2022[53] former US President Obama highlighted the sheer severity of the situation and the degree of unpreparedness both he and the White House had in understanding the vulnerability of democracies to weaponised information through AI and technologies.

David, Lord Puttnam, former celebrated film producer and member of the House of Lords, chaired a House of Lords Special Inquiry committee into the impact of digital technology on our democratic processes, which led to its report: *Digital Technology and the Resurrection of Trust* in 2020.[54]

In his valedictory lecture in October 2021, he expressed its conclusions in this way:

I believed and continue to believe that the 'resurrection' of our capacity to trust each other, and the systems through which we receive information – the same information on which we base many of the most important decisions of our lives – is fundamental to our survival as a coherent society.[55]

In 2021 an investigation by ProPublica and the Washington Post found that user groups on popular social media platforms swelled in activity, with at least 650,000 individual posts attacking the legitimacy of Joe Biden's victory, between the Election Day in 2020 and the US Capitol riots in January 2021, with many calling for executions or other political violence.[56] Revelations of this nature were quickly followed by evidence to both the US Senate and the UK Joint Committee on the Draft Online Safety Bill of clear failures by social media platforms in preventing harmful information being disseminated through their channels during political events.

Former Meta employee Frances Haugen gave damning testimony to the US Senate and to the UK parliament's Joint Committee on the Draft Online Safety Bill. She released tens of thousands of internal Facebook documents outlining the firm's failure to keep harmful content off its platforms and accused the company of putting 'astronomical profits before people'.[57]

The use of technology, AI or otherwise, in such a manner continues a long trend of targeted manipulation. For some time now, free speech and anti-disinformation campaigners Avaaz[58] have tracked the virality of political fake news stories on social media platforms and many of the effects caused. Recent investigative reports carried out by the group include tracking a tidal wave of targeted social media disinformation during the 2020 Presidential Election with a volume sufficient to reach every eligible voter in the US at least once.

Beyond the capability of AI to generate misinformation and disinformation, there is equally a heightened risk in its ability to target users and individuals based on data points from their own lives. In a previous world, political advertising was based on 'larger' more obvious points of data, including typical demographic data such as age, profession, income, education levels, and any obvious links to possibilities of children within the associated household. Profiles were mainly based on general abstract profiles of users.

The use of AI allows targeting to be much more subtle and far more influential. Termed 'Surveillance Capitalism' by Shoshana Zuboff,[59] AI is able to make use of far greater details from the life of an individual. Do they, for example: Have a trend of purchasing from specific high-end stores; Is there a trend of purchasing during sale periods; Is their most common payment method a credit or debit card? … and so on. All of these data points can be sold to companies capable of synthesising information and targeting political campaigns and advertisements on social platforms and other online technologies – including advertisement on the apps used on mobile phones.

From these data points, a specific data profile is created, and targeted advertisements and recommended posts are released in a relentless bombardment on the particular individual or groups. This can be used to alter the way we vote, especially with disinformation. Where the algorithm identifies points of particularly strong engagement, then extreme or exaggerated content is often used to amplify engagement, and outrage is often encouraged. Echo-chambers are quickly created and opinions and emotions of the targeted individual are fuelled and amplified.

Political algorithmic targeting of this nature is potentially more effective against swing voters or those with no clearly identifiable political digital profile. As seen in the case of the 2016 UK Brexit vote, many who were undecided or unclear on what way to vote were heavily targeted through algorithm-backed political advertisement and posts, often raising extreme concerns that would strike at the heart of the sensitivities of an undecided voter, such as unchecked immigration.

A leading article in the Observer in 2018 reflecting on its exposé of the activities of Cambridge Analytica asserted:

swing voters are targeted based on narrow issues, using false claims or under-the-radar dog-whistling that are not subjected to public scrutiny. Meanwhile, voters seen as already decided, or insignificant to the result, go ignored.[60]

So how do countries, particularly those with strongly held democratic values, govern the use of AI in such a manner that mitigates or prevents these harms and retains trust in the digital world?

The UK has sought to investigate this very question through several parliamentary enquiries. In 2019, for example, the House of Commons Digital Culture Media and Sport Select Committee report into Disinformation and Fake News[61] made several recommendations regarding restrictions on political advertising, data use, and targeting during elections and on foreign influence in political campaigns. Some time afterwards in 2021, the same question arose during the work of the Joint Committee on the Online Safety Bill as they investigated societal harms caused through online technologies, including those leveraging algorithms and generative capabilities.

Similar questions arose during the work of the Joint Committee on the Online Safety Bill as they investigated societal harms caused through online technologies, including those leveraging algorithms, generative capabilities, and the harms of misinformation. In their report, published in December 2021,[62] the Committee concluded that:

Disinformation and misinformation surrounding elections are a risk to democracy. Disinformation which aims to disrupt elections must be addressed by legislation. If the Government decides that the Online Safety Bill is not the appropriate place to do so, then it should use the Elections Bill which is currently making its way through Parliament.

Tackling societal harms caused by misinformation and disinformation is not straightforward, however, particularly so for multiparty democracies. There is, for example, an evident tension between protecting individuals from harmful information and the inherent right to freedom of expression. A careful balancing act is therefore required in order to – within the realm of practical capability – tackle what would be considered 'harmful' information, without overly restricting society's ability to share and digest content online.

For those who believe in the inalienability of free speech, the harm principle enunciated by John Stuart Mill in his philosophical work *On Liberty*[63] is still valid after over 150 years: People should be free to act however they wish unless their actions cause harm to somebody else. Article 10 of the European Convention on Human Rights[64] gives that right as regards freedom of expression, and in the US similar protection to free speech is contained within the First Amendment to the Constitution.[65]

To square this circle, the Joint Committee report proposed a content-neutral safety-by-design approach, where specific design requirements, such as increasing transparency, countering algorithmic power, and de-viralising and diversifying content through 'friction' mitigation would be mandated prior to their deployment. The Committee heard evidence that this is a proven way to preserve free speech while limiting free reach of content that poses societal harm at scale.

For example, it heard that a simple change, introducing more friction into sharing on social media platforms, would have the same effect on the spread of misinformation and disinformation as an entire third-party fact-checking system. The Joint Committee believed that these could play a vital part in tackling content and activity that creates a risk of societal harm especially the spread of disinformation.

But assuming that such governance mandates are put into place, how do these become measures that can be acted upon in the effective mitigation of AI-specific risks to democratic and societal values? And furthermore, which arm of government (or business) is responsible for enforcement?

The long-delayed 2020 report of the UK Intelligence and Security Committee (ICS) on Russian interference[66] demonstrated the urgency of these questions of governance in finding that the UK, and indeed other allied democracies, were the targets of state-sponsored disinformation campaigns and political interference. The US Senate Intelligence Committee in 2020 similarly found that the US and its allies were targets for AI-enabled political interference.[67]

The ICS questioned whether electoral law is sufficiently up to date, given 'the move from physical billboards to online, micro-targeted political campaigning' and whether the Electoral Commission, responsible for regulation of electoral activities, had sufficient powers to ensure the security of democratic processes where hostile state threats are involved.

From evidence given to the UK Joint Committee during their inquiry, accountabilities are unclear. Rather surprisingly, the UK's own security services considered that they did not have primary responsibility for defending democracy in the UK from such harms. The Joint Committee, however, concluded that responsibility did fall within the statutory remit of the security services to protect national security, in particular against threats from sabotage and the activities of foreign powers intended to undermine parliamentary democracy.

It does not necessarily, however, address instances where ties to foreign powers are not present or clear and the source of misinformation activity is closer to home. It is equally plausible, for example, that organisations, ostensibly not linked to political parties, seek to influence people to vote for a particular candidate who is particularly friendly to their interests. There is no doubt that the tightening of electoral law is required as part of the solution.

In 2021 the UK's Committee on Standards in Public Life[68] made several recommendations regarding digital and social media campaigning. In particular it recommended that the government should change the law to require parties and campaigners to provide the Electoral Commission with more detailed invoices from their digital suppliers. For targeted advertisements, this should include information relating to the messages used in those campaigns, which parts of the country they were targeted at, and how much was spent on each campaign. It also recommended that the government require social media platforms that permit election advertisements in the UK to create advertisement libraries that include information such as precise figures for amounts spent, rather than ranges, who paid for the advertisement, for targeted adverts, information about the intended target audience of the advert, and the types of people who actually saw the advert. In line with the principle of no foreign interference in UK elections, they also said that the government should legislate to ban foreign organisations or individuals from buying campaign advertising in the UK.

Given all the strong recommendations from these committees and the potential ways in which the UK government (and other democratic governments) could mitigate the potential for AI to pose substantial risks to the underpinning rights and values that uphold the democratic process, the questions arise as to why more extensive safeguards were not included in the UK's recently updated elections legislation to take account of the mounting evidence and concerns about the impact of AI? Equally, why have other democratic governments failed to implement protective measures in the face of a rapidly developing technological environment?

At least within the UK, certain changes were made in response to those raised with respect to electoral legislation which, while not explicitly targeted at AI, did provide some positive steps towards governance of its impacts on democracy and democratic values. For example, the UK's Electoral Commission was provided additional powers to enforce 'digital imprints' on campaign materials which informed individuals of who paid for and who produced certain content online. This is restricted, however, to instances where politically affiliated parties and organisations are involved and therefore is of little value in direct action against bad actors. Potential impacts on democracy could be mitigated further if the UK government were to implement many of the other recommendations proposed by the Electoral Commission, including minimum standards of transparency in how the recommendation algorithms work and from whom content is originating. Through a combination of the Online Safety Act of 2023 and the National Security Act of the same year, internet platforms in future however will need to carry out risk assessments for and mitigate the possibility of users encountering content which is illegal under a new foreign interference offence. This is broadly, interference with public functions or intent to manipulate how or whether a person participates in a political or legal process.

The UK government, also in 2019, did set up what is called the Counter Disinformation Unit (CDU),[69] recently renamed the National Security Online Information Team which now sits with the new Department for Science, Innovation and Technology. Its purpose in the government's words 'is to understand disinformation narratives and attempts to artificially manipulate the information environment to ensure that the government understands the scope and reach of harmful misinformation and disinformation and can take appropriate action.'

While it is welcome so far as it goes, whether the CDU will prove in any way adequate to the task of tackling the threat to democracy of misinformation is doubtful since the CDU is expressly stated to focus on content targeted at UK audiences which poses a risk to public health, public safety, or national security, not on democratic processes.

The impact of generative AI

The recent rapid development of generative AI and its capabilities in creating virtually undetectable fake images, audio, and footage has created an even greater threat to authentic democratic discourse. It has been predicted that 2024 will be a significant challenge for democracy in the face of AI.[70] This is particularly so owing to the sheer number of democratic elections taking place in a regulatory environment that is only just coming to terms with generative AI. Over 70 countries with a combined population of over

4 billion are expected to vote in an array of presidential, parliamentary, European, federal, state, and municipal elections.[71] In many cases, this will be the first occasion on which many of the world's biggest democracies will have held a vote since generative AI tools and platforms, such as ChatGPT and Midjourney, took the world by storm.

These concerns are by no means unfounded. Professor Ciaran Martin, the former head of the National Cyber Security Centre and current professor of Oxford's Blavatnik School of Government has said that AI could make it much more difficult to see what is 'true and reliable' as it becomes capable of impersonating real people. In particular, Professor Martin highlights that AI has made it far easier to make fake content appear legitimate, and then easier to disseminate it at scale. He has since predicted that it will become far more difficult in future to determine what sources to trust and what information is actually reliable.[72]

Then we have the example of the Slovakian Parliamentary elections in 2023. During this process, fake audio recordings of Michal Šimečka, the leader of the liberal Progressive Slovakia Party, created by readily available generative AI, were posted, apparently discussing how to rig the election. Mr Šimečka went on to lose the election to the populist pro-Moscow Smer-SSD party.[73] Not long after this in the UK a fake audio of the Leader of the Opposition, Sir Keir Starmer, surfaced just before Labour's autumn conference, which appeared to show him swearing at members of his staff.[74]

Concern has not been confined to Slovakia. A YouGov survey taken in January 2024 of UK members of parliament (MPs) showed that an overwhelming majority view the rise of AI-generated content as a top concern.[75]

Several approaches to mitigating this risk have been considered globally. For example, where AI has generated content, or where content has been created through AI in a manner that may convince individuals that they are interacting with a human or human-made content, a suitable disclaimer or warning could be included. Individuals would at the very least be able to identify when AI has been involved and could then determine what level of trust to give the information. This is useful when working with individuals and organisations that act within the confines of the law. It does not, however, offer much protection from the work of bad actors intent on deception.

Other options include the use of technology to identify metadata embedded in text and images and to determine whether something has been created through the use of generative AI. While this is a promising option if it is able to be implemented comprehensively across AI works, the technological tools to ensure this, such as watermarking to detect deepfakes, and otherwise identify when dealing with AI-created materials are still in their relative infancy and in a sense we are already in a race against deepfake tools as they grow in sophistication and reduced levels of detectability.

There are already a number of projects that aspire to tackle the problem through these authentication technologies. There is the work of Logically. AI, for example,[76] which assesses foreign interference, authenticity, attribution, and provenance checking through organisations such as Full Fact or metadata embedding tools developed by the Content Authenticity Initiative (CAI).[77] As with detection software, this is still in relative infancy and is only able to deal with the very tip of the iceberg.

It is equally not sufficient to rely exclusively on the actions of the government. As the former Director of GCHQ, the UK's digital and cybersecurity service, Sir Jeremy Fleming has said, '*we must make sure that we stay true to our values, those that have made our systems and democracies so successful and will do so in the future.*'[78]

It is clear that even the combination of regulation and technology cannot deal with all the issues of misinformation, disinformation, and deepfakery.

In the face of these technological threats it is clear – not least from our politicians – that we need a collective response to the question, 'are we doing everything necessary to preserve the democratic values and processes afforded to us and the fundamental rights that such values and processes protect?'

Effective governance of AI risks in the context of democratic values and processes requires steps to build democratic resilience. In addition to technical and regulatory measures, there needs to be, as Lord Puttnam's Select Committee report identified, direct and comprehensive public engagement to support digital literacy at all levels of society.

Digital literacy is the ability both to use technology and to comprehend the impact that it has on our lives and address the vast literacy skills and knowledge gap that leaves a population and society at risk of harms in the digital era. Governments would be wise to (where they have not already) develop and implement digital and media literacy strategy to level up society's understanding of the potential risk of interacting with the digital world. This aspect is also discussed in Chapter 6.

4 Public Sector Adoption: Live Facial Recognition, Lethal Autonomous Weapons, and Ethical Use

Automated decision-making and frontier AI adoption in the public sector

Over the past few years, we have seen a substantial increase in the adoption of algorithmic decision-making (ADM) and prediction across central and local government. Public sector bodies in several countries are now using algorithms, AI, and similar methods in their administrative functions to assess need and make decisions such as on tax, and in a whole variety of social security areas, such as benefits and welfare provision.

As a result, the use of algorithms in government – and more specifically, algorithmic decision-making – has come under increasing scrutiny. The debate became more intense after the UK government's disastrous attempt in 2020 to use an algorithm to determine A-level and GCSE grades in lieu of exams, which had been cancelled due to the COVID pandemic.

This is what the FT had to say in August 2020 after the Ofqual Exam debacle where students were subjected to what has been described as unfair and unaccountable decision-making over their GCSE and A-level grades after traditional examinations were cancelled because of the COVID pandemic.

The soundtrack of school students marching through Britain's streets shouting 'f*** the algorithm' captured the sense of outrage surrounding the botched awarding of A-level exam grades this year. But the students' anger towards a disembodied computer algorithm is misplaced. This was a human failure…

It concluded:

Given the severe erosion of public trust in the government's use of technology, it might now be advisable to subject all automated decision-making systems to critical scrutiny by independent experts… As ever, technology in itself is neither good nor bad. But it is certainly not neutral. The more we deploy automated decision-making systems, the smarter we must become in considering how best to use them and in scrutinising their outcomes.[79]

The ante has been further raised, as the Ada Lovelace Institute have recently identified,[80] by the 'retail' use of so-called frontier AI applications, typically generative AI and LLMs, by individual staff in the public sector to carry out a range of tasks. This may often be from the best of motives but carries severe risks of lack of quality control.

Before the large-scale advent of generative AI an investigation by the Guardian in late 2019 showed that some 140 of 408 councils in the UK were using privately developed algorithmic 'risk assessment' tools, particularly to determine eligibility for benefits and to calculate entitlements, despite concerns about their reliability.[81] According to the Guardian, nearly a year later in 2020 that figure had increased to half of local councils in England, Wales, and Scotland, many of them without any consultation with the public on their use.

Similarly, Data Justice Lab research in late 2018[82] showed that 53 out of 96 local authorities and about a quarter of police authorities were now using algorithms for prediction, risk assessment, and assistance in decision-making.

Big Brother Watch's Poverty Panopticon of 2021 further illustrated the widespread use of algorithmic decision-making in the public sector in the UK. It identified that:

- Approximately 1 in 3 local authorities risk-score people who receive housing benefit and council tax support when they apply, using opaque, privately developed algorithms, covering more than 540,000 people.
- Approximately 1 in 3 local authorities and more than 1 in 3 housing associations run predictive analytics to assess whether

social housing occupants will keep up with rent payments, adding up to 1.6 million tenancies.

- Some large local authorities use bigger predictive systems that can model who is at risk of homelessness (Newcastle, Maidstone, Cornwall, Croydon, Haringey); others use similar systems to model children at risk of harm (Hillingdon, Bristol); while others can model general financial vulnerability (Barking and Dagenham) with at least 250,000 people's data being processed by huge predictive tools.
- The Department for Work and Pensions conducts risk modelling of housing benefit recipients on a regular basis to predict who poses the highest fraud/error risk due to change of circumstance, and passes this data to local authorities.

This has on occasion led to bad outcomes that could have been avoided. In particular, we have had the Harm Assessment Risk Tool – HART – system used by Durham police to predict reoffending, which was shown by Big Brother Watch[83] to have serious flaws in the way the use of profiling data introduces bias and discrimination and dubious predictions.

Central government use has been particularly opaque. HMRC, the Ministry of Justice, and the DWP are the highest spenders on digital, data, and algorithmic services. A key example of ADM use in central government is the DWP's universal credit system, which was designed to be digital by default from the beginning. The Child Poverty Action Group, in its study, *Computer Says 'No!'*, in 2019[84] showed that those accessing their online account were not being given adequate explanation as to how their entitlement was calculated.

The UN Special Rapporteur on extreme poverty and human rights, Philip Alston, looked at the UK's universal credit system and said in a statement afterwards:

Government is increasingly automating itself with the use of data and new technology tools, including AI. Evidence shows that the human rights of the poorest and most vulnerable are especially at risk in such

49

contexts. A major issue with the development of new technologies by the UK government is a lack of transparency.[85]

The Joint Council for the Welfare of Immigrants (JCWI) and campaigning organisation Foxglove joined forces in 2020 to sue the Home Office over an allegedly discriminatory algorithmic system – the so-called 'streaming tool' – used to screen migration applications.[86] This was the first successful legal challenge to an algorithmic decision system in the UK, although before having to defend the system in court, the Home Office decided to scrap the algorithm.

Internationally the use of algorithms is even more extensive and controversial – particularly in the US. One such system is the New York Police Department's 'Patternizr',[87] a tool that the NYPD has designed to identify potential future patterns of criminal activity but has raised questions around AI bias. Others which have been criticised on the same basis include Northpointe's COMPAS risk assessment programme in Florida mentioned earlier, and the InterRAI care assessment algorithm in Arkansas.[88]

Cathy O'Neil's *Weapons of Math Destruction* (2016) and Hannah Fry's *Hello World* (2018), mentioned in our introduction, warn us of the dangers of replication of historical bias in algorithmic decision-making. It is clear that failure to properly regulate these systems risks embedding bias and inaccuracy. Even when not relying on ADM alone, the impact of automated decision-making systems across an entire population can be immense in terms of potential discrimination, breach of privacy, access to justice, and other rights.

Some of the current issues with ADM were identified in the House of Lords Select Committee Report, *AI in the UK: Ready Willing and Able?* in 2018[89] which the author chaired. In the report, the Committee indicated that:

it is not acceptable to deploy any artificial intelligence system which could have a substantial impact on an individual's life, unless it can generate a full and satisfactory explanation for the decisions it will take.

It was also already clear from the evidence that the AI Select Committee took, which dealt with automated individual decision-making, that UK law does not provide sufficient protection to those subject to ADM.

Currently Article 22 of UK GDPR[90] provides that:

The data subject shall have the right not to be subject to a decision based solely on automated processing, including profiling, which produces legal effects concerning him or her or similarly affects him or her.

However, few highly significant decisions are fully automated – often, they are used as decision support, for example in detecting child abuse.

The Science and Technology Select Committee Report *Algorithms in Decision-Making* of May 2018,[91] made extensive recommendations in this respect. It urged the adoption of a legally enforceable 'right to explanation' that allows citizens to find out how machine-learning programs reach decisions affecting them – and potentially challenge their results. It also called for a minister to be appointed with responsibility for making sure that the Nolan standards of public life are observed for algorithm use in local authorities and the public sector and for departments to publicly declare where and how they use them.

Subsequently, in 2019, a report by the Law Society of England and Wales[92] published about the use of algorithms in the criminal justice system expressed concern, and recommended measures for oversight, registration, and mitigation of risks in the justice system.

Even when not using ADM solely, the impact of an automated decision-making system across an entire population can be immense in terms of potential discrimination, breach of privacy, access to justice, and other rights. In 2020, the Committee on Standards in Public Life decided to carry out a review of AI in the public sector to understand its implications for the Nolan principles – the Principles of Public Life which are ethical standards those working in the public sector are expected to adhere to[93] and to examine whether UK government policy was up to the task of upholding standards as AI is rolled out across our public services. The committee chair, Lord Evans of Weardale, said on publishing the report:[94]

Artificial intelligence – and in particular, machine learning – will transform the way public sector organisations make decisions and deliver public services. Demonstrating high standards will help realise the huge potential benefits of AI in public service delivery. However, it is clear that the public need greater reassurance about the use of AI in the public sector. Public sector organisations are not sufficiently transparent about their use of AI and it is too difficult to find out where machine learning is currently being used in government.[95]

It found that, despite the GDPR,[96] the data ethics framework, the OECD principles, and the guidelines for using artificial intelligence in the public sector, the Nolan principles of openness, accountability, and objectivity were not, but should be, embedded in AI governance in the public sector.

The Committee's report recommended a number of solutions, including greater transparency by public bodies in the use of algorithms, new guidance to ensure that algorithmic decision-making abides by equalities law, the creation of a single coherent regulatory framework to govern this area, the formation of a body to advise existing regulators on relevant issues, and proper routes of redress for citizens who feel decisions are unfair.

In 2020 ministers commissioned the AI adoption review, which was designed to assess the ways that artificial intelligence could be deployed across Whitehall and the wider public sector. Yet the government blocked the full publication of the report and provided only a heavily redacted version.[97] The use of AI and algorithms in government in the UK is still opaque.

There has in fact been no shortage of government guidance applicable to AI systems available. This includes guidance on using AI in the public sector in 2019.[98] Then it introduced an Ethics, Transparency and Accountability Framework for Automated Decision-Making,[99] which is a seven-point framework to help government departments with the 'safe, sustainable and ethical use of automated or algorithmic decision-making systems.'

Perhaps the most helpful guidance has been provided by the Equality and Human Rights Commission in its *Artificial Intelligence: checklist for public bodies in England*,[100] setting out how public bodies that do not have a specific duty to prepare or publish an equality impact assessment (EIA) to think about what they need to do to comply with the Public Sector Equality Duty when adopting AI systems to prevent discrimination and bias against groups with protected characteristics.

There has even been growing recognition of the need for greater central and local government transparency in its use of AI and algorithmic systems. This matters because people are being harmed and discriminated against in cases where public bodies make algorithmic predictions about them without their knowledge. We need much greater transparency about current deployment, plans for adoption, and compliance mechanisms.

In 2021 the UK government introduced its Algorithmic Transparency Recording Standard,[101] subsequently updated in 2023, designed to help public sector organisations provide clear information about the algorithmic tools they use, and why they're using them. On being asked in June 2023 about the status of compliance with the Standard, however, the UK Cabinet Office minister responsible responded in answer to a written question:

It is currently being rolled out more widely across the public sector with a view to embedding it into internal governance processes and increasing compliance.

but...

Enshrining the Standard into law at this point of maturity might hinder the ability to ensure it remains relevant in a rapidly developing technology field. We remain committed to reevaluating our position on legislative change in the future, once the policy and the Standard have matured further.[102]

This is another demonstration that the adoption of mechanisms to ensure compliance in government with guidance is painfully slow. There is still no enforceable obligation for transparency in the form of a public register of use of ADM. By contrast, a public register of use of ADM has been instituted by the Federal Canadian government – via its Directive on

Automated Decision-Making[103] and a number of municipal authorities such as Amsterdam and Helsinki.

Both the *Mind the Gap*[104] report from the Institute for the Future of Work in 2020, which proposed an Accountability for Algorithms Act, and the Ada Lovelace Institute paper, *Can Algorithms Ever Make the Grade?* called for a public register of algorithms, and independent external scrutiny to ensure the efficacy and accuracy of algorithmic systems.

In 2022, to show what is possible, I introduced a private members' Bill – the Public Authority Algorithm Bill – which was inspired by the Canadian directive. Sadly, this did not progress very far, but it was designed to ensure that decisions made by public authorities – local and national – are fully transparent and properly assessed for the impact they have on the rights of the individual citizen.

It mandated the government to draw up a framework for an impact assessment which follows a set of principles laid out in the Bill so that (a) decisions made in and by a public authority are responsible and comply with procedural fairness and due process requirements, and its duties under the Equality Act, (b) impacts of algorithms on administrative decisions are assessed, and negative outcomes are minimised, and (c) data and information on the use of automated decision systems in public authorities are made available to the public. It would apply in general to any automated decision system developed or procured by a public authority other than the security services.

It is instructive, however, to read the government response to the House of Lords Justice and Home Affairs Committee's report *Technology Rules?* in 2022,[105] which despite expressing the need for responsible, ethical, legitimate, necessary, and proportionate and safe AI displays a marked reluctance to be subject to specific regulation in this area.

Procurement and contract conditions are powerful and practical instruments for public sector authorities to ensure that AI-enabled systems comply with fundamental rights and democratic values. In June 2020, the UK government published *Guidelines for Artificial Intelligence (AI) Procurement*[106] which were developed by the UK government's Office for AI, in collaboration with the World Economic Forum Centre Government Digital Service, Government Commercial Function and Crown Commercial

Service. The UK was trumpeted as the first government to pilot these procurement guidelines. The purpose of the guidelines is to provide central government departments and other public sector bodies with a set of guiding principles for purchasing AI technology. It also covers guidance on tackling challenges that may occur during the procurement process.

One of the most disappointing aspects of current UK procurement law, however, is the lack of mandatory connection to the guidelines. Despite the passing of a new Procurement Act in 2023[107] the current government has resisted setting out any of the ethical rules that should underpin our public procurement of technology in binding legislation or regulation. Without any legal duty backing up these various guidelines it is unlikely that they will add up to very much beyond aspiration. Alongside a legal duty to adhere to procurement guidance, standard contractual clauses for ethical AI procurement should also be developed.

As regards the use of frontier AI in the public sector, there is no doubt that in the light of its now widespread use, current procurement rules cannot ensure the quality and good governance of AI systems deployed. The risks may appear to be the same as for ordinary consumers and worthy of regulation and guidance in any event but, given the context in which they are being used – by public servants for a public purpose – even greater risk mitigation is needed.

The Ada Lovelace Institute in their policy briefing *AI in the Public Sector*[108] say that there is evidence of foundation model applications (such as ChatGPT) being used on an informal basis by individual civil servants and local authority staff. Formal use of foundation models in the public sector is currently limited to demos, prototypes, and proofs of concept.

As they say, in further adopting these models in the public sector, there are risks in over-reliance on private-sector providers, including a potential lack of alignment between applications developed for a wider range of private-sector clients and the needs of the public sector. In particular, they consider public-sector clients:

- are more likely to deal with highly sensitive data
- have higher standards of robustness

- require higher levels of transparency and explainability in important decisions around welfare, healthcare, education, and other public services.

In this light it is clear overall that the position regarding deployment of specific AI systems by government is still very unsatisfactory. Given the lack of a legal duty on the public sector to adhere to ethical principles, the Ada Lovelace Institute's suggestions for the governance regime needed for frontier AI use in their policy briefing referred to earlier have wider application and should be adapted for the adoption of AI in the public sector more generally. The following, for instance, could and should be mandatory for all AI systems in the UK public sector with a clear compliance mechanism.

- Mandating independent third-party audits for all foundation models used in the public sector, whether developed in-house or externally procured.
- Incorporating meaningful public engagement in the governance of foundation models, particularly in public-facing applications.
- Piloting new use cases before wider rollout, in order to identify risks and challenges.
- Monitoring AI applications on an ongoing basis.
- Ensuring adherence to the Algorithmic Transparency Recording Standard across the public sector.

Recently a group of UK civil society organisations led by the Public Law Project in response to the UK government's Pro Innovation AI White Paper[109] of March 2023, in what they called Key Principles for an Alternative White Paper,[110] proposed that public sector AI use should specifically be subject to regulation in line with the following principles. They asserted that:

- Transparency must be mandatory.
- There must be clear mechanisms for accountability at every stage.

- The public should be consulted about new automated decision-making (ADM) tools before they are deployed by government.
- There must be a specialist regulator to enforce the regulatory regime and to ensure that people can seek redress when things go wrong.
- Uses of AI that threaten fundamental rights should be prohibited.

Big Brother Watch has also suggested we need to:

- Amend the Data Protection Act to ensure that any decisions involving automated processing that engage rights protected under the Human Rights Act 1998 are required ultimately to be human decisions with meaningful human input.
- Introduce a requirement for mandatory bias-testing of any algorithms, automated processes, or AI software used by the police and criminal justice system in decision-making processes.
- Prohibit the use of predictive policing systems that have the potential to reinforce discriminatory and unfair policing patterns.

Effective redress for complaints about the use of AI in the public sector in decision-making is of crucial importance too. This will inevitably give rise to complaints requiring specialist skills beyond sectoral or data knowledge. This is especially true of public sector ombudsman services who are tasked with dealing with complaints about algorithmic decision-making.

Live facial recognition

Even less reassuring is the governance regime applying to the use of the specific technology of live facial recognition in the public sector, such as in policing where government – the Home Office, in particular – has displayed ever greater enthusiasm for its deployment.

Despite the efforts of parliamentarians and organisations such as the Ada Lovelace Institute, there has been no recognition at all that new regulation for intrusive AI technology such as live facial recognition is needed, indeed quite the reverse. As a result, in the UK, we are still engaged in a major debate on the deployment of live facial recognition technology – the use of biometrics and AI – in policing, schools, and criminal justice. Many campaigning organisations have real concerns that we are approaching the surveillance state, particularly now that major retailers are introducing it into their stores to identify shoplifters. This technology and its use has been described by the Biometrics and Surveillance Camera Commissioner for England and Wales until October 2023, Professor Fraser Sampson, as 'increasingly intrusive'.[111]

In the successful appeal of Councillor Ed Bridges, the Court of Appeal case on police use of live facial recognition issued in August 2020,[112] it ruled that South Wales Police's (SWP's) use of automated facial recognition (AFR) had not in fact been in accordance with the law on several grounds including in relation to certain European human rights convention rights; data protection legislation; and the public sector equality duty.

In particular, the Court of Appeal held that SWP's use of facial recognition constituted an unlawful breach of Article 8 (right to privacy) of the European Human Rights convention as it was not in accordance with law. The Court held that:

> the fundamental deficiencies... in the legal framework currently in place relate to two areas of concern. The first is what was called the 'who question' at the hearing before us. The second is the 'where question'. In relation to both of those questions too much discretion is currently left to individual police officers. It is not clear who can be placed on the watchlist nor is it clear that there are any criteria for determining where AFR can be deployed.

As the Court of Appeal noted: 'Biometric data enables the unique identification of individuals with some accuracy. It is this which distinguishes it from many other forms of data.' The Court of Appeal also agreed that South Wales Police had failed to meet their Public Sector Equality Duty, which requires public bodies and others carrying out public functions to have due regard to the need to eliminate bias.

The 2022 report of the House of Lords Justice and Home Affairs Committee, *Technology Rules?*, mentioned above, noted the complicated institutional landscape around the adoption of this kind of technology and emphasised the need for public trust. It recommended:

- a stronger legal framework with primary legislation that embodies general principles supported by detailed regulation
- a single national regulatory body
- minimum scientific standards
- local or regional ethics committees put on a statutory basis.

As the report by Matthew Ryder KC[113] commissioned by the Ada Lovelace Institute *The independent legal review of the governance of biometric data in England and Wales in 2022* pointed out, neither House of Parliament has ever adequately considered or rigorously scrutinised AFR. We remain in the precarious position of police forces dictating the debate – taking it firmly out of the hands of elected parliamentarians and instead marking their own homework.

A range of studies have shown facial recognition technology disproportionately misidentifies women and BAME people meaning that people from these groups are more likely to be wrongly stopped and questioned by police, and to have their images retained as the result of a false match. To date, of 3337 facial recognition flags by South Wales Police and the Metropolitan Police Service, just 362 have been true matches, while over 65 people have faced wrongful interventions from police officers as a result of a false facial recognition flag.

The independent report conducted into the Met's 2019 trial of live facial recognition technology by Professor Peter Fussey and Dr Daragh Murray of the University of Essex's Human Rights Centre concluded that the technology was only accurate on 19% of occasions and had severe operational shortcomings that would be unlikely to hold up in court.[114]

Although the Metropolitan Police Service relies on a study by the National Physical Laboratory[115] as regards the accuracy of facial recognition technology, in terms of matches across different demographic groups when used at a particular threshold setting, this does not address legality issues. Even on technical grounds it is open to challenge since the accuracy and precision (true positive identification rate) of the technology depends on the operational settings chosen and even a small lowering of identification thresholds can have a profound effect on the number of false positives in live settings, with severe consequences for the incidence of arrest, stop, and search. Furthermore, there is no transparency about the settings chosen.

The UK is now the most camera-surveilled country in the Western world. London remains the third most surveilled city in the world, with 73 surveillance cameras for every thousand people. A survey carried out by Sampson's predecessor, Tony Porter, shortly before stepping down found, in 2020, that at that time there were over 6000 systems and 80,000 cameras in operation in England and Wales across 183 local authorities.[116]

The ubiquity of surveillance cameras, which can be retrofitted with facial recognition software and fed into police databases, means that there is already an apparatus in place for large-scale intrusive surveillance, which can easily be augmented by the widespread adoption of facial recognition technology. Indeed, many surveillance cameras in the UK already have advanced capabilities such as biometric identification, behavioural analysis, anomaly detection, item/clothing recognition, vehicle recognition, and profiling. The risks presented by continued expansion of facial recognition include the use of this technology not only through the pre-existing CCTV network but also through body-worn video, enabling passive, real-time monitoring of us all – entirely without suspicion and without our knowledge or consent.

Professor Sampson's duties have included overseeing police use of DNA and fingerprints and monitoring the use of surveillance cameras in public spaces in England, Wales, and Northern Ireland. During an appearance before Parliament's Joint Committee on Human Rights in February 2023,[117] Sampson noted there was a 'non-deletion culture' in UK policing when it came to the retention of biometric information – which includes facial images. Much of this biometric information, as Computer Weekly has reported, is now either held or is being moved to public cloud infrastructure, which opens data subjects up to a number of risks.

There is also concern that transferring personal data, including biometrics, to the US – a jurisdiction with demonstrably lower data protection standards – could in turn negatively impact people's data rights to rectification, erasure, and not be subject to automated decision-making. In December 2020, for example, a Computer Weekly investigation revealed that UK police forces were unlawfully processing more than one million people's personal data – including biometrics – on the public cloud service Microsoft 365, after failing to comply with key contractual and processing requirements within Part Three of the Data Protection Act 2018, such as restrictions placed on international transfers.[118]

Professor Sampson has raised concerns about the use of cameras employed for this surveillance and data capture supplied by companies whose governments do not subscribe to GDPR equivalent duties, such as the Chinese company Hikvision.[119] To make matters worse, in the new Data Protection and Digital Information Bill,[120] going through parliament at the time of writing, the separate and independent role of the Biometrics and Surveillance Camera Commissioner is being abolished together with a number of their duties such as the production of a Surveillance Camera Code of Conduct. This has been described in a recent report from the Centre for Research into Information, Surveillance and Privacy (CRISP)[121] as a 'worrying vacuum' in government plans to safeguard the public, which will leave the UK without proper oversight just when advances in artificial intelligence (AI) and other technologies mean that they are needed more than ever.

Concerns have also been raised about the potential use by public authorities of US databases such as that created by Clearview AI which unlawfully 'scraped' some 3 billion images from the web to create it. They were fined more than £7.5m, and UK data held by them was ordered to be deleted.[122]

Outside the public sector, it is clear that the UK's Information Commissioner's Office (ICO), where possible, needs to use existing data protection powers to protect our rights in the UK from a range of privacy incursions across many sectors. Two recent decisions made by the ICO are particularly concerning and appear to put the interests of private companies above the data rights of the public. Facial recognition companies PimEyes and Facewatch have both been the subject of detailed legal complaints, which have outlined how the companies' systems violate the data rights and privacy of potentially millions of people in the UK. The ICO's decision not to take firm enforcement action over these companies' failures to respect data protection law and to safeguard sensitive personal data is deeply worrying.[123]

PimEyes is a publicly available facial recognition search engine that allows anybody with an internet connection to search for images of any individual across the open internet. The technology can link a face to a name, address, job, and political and religious beliefs with ease, through the contextual information surfaced by a PimEyes search. Disturbingly, journalists and campaigners have uncovered a series of examples of the technology being used to harass and track women.

As regards the ICO's investigation into Facewatch, a company that provides live facial recognition to British retailers, it found it had violated data protection law on eight counts. That is, tens of thousands of people – perhaps more – had been unlawfully scanned. But worryingly, the ICO declined to take further regulatory action – such as fining Facewatch for those breaches.

The Baden-Württemberg data protection authority in Germany by contrast has initiated legal proceedings against PimEyes,[124] citing concerns over the company's processing of biometric data, the lack of consent from data subjects, an opt-out option that places the onus on the data subject to protect their data from being made accessible to an indefinite number of people, and the possibility of third-party abuse.

Since the ICO's Facewatch decision was publicised, there have been reports of new and suggested uses of facial recognition surveillance, including bouncers in bars using live facial recognition to identify those accused of 'disorder' and the proposed use of the passport photo database for facial recognition searches in relation to low-level crime.

The subject of live facial recognition technology has been raised many times in parliamentary questions and debates – even a private members' Bill – over the last five years, and it has been the subject of a number of enquiries. The House of Commons Science and Technology Committee has, over time, been highly critical of the lack of progress made by the government in the areas of forensic market sustainability, laboratory accreditation, biometrics governance, and custody image management, and of the government intentions regarding the introduction of a clarified legislative framework for AFR technology.[125]

Guidance (*Live Facial Recognition Authorised Professional Practice*) from the National College of Policing was issued in 2022, albeit with minimal consultation, and it immediately attracted criticism.[126] As Big Brother Watch have said, the guidance is extraordinarily permissive, setting virtually no limitations on police use of the technology.

With a lack of a legal basis for the use of this technology, the guidance is regarded as insufficient by organisations as wide ranging as Liberty, Big Brother Watch, the Ada Lovelace Institute, the former Information Commissioner, both the then current and former Biometrics and Surveillance Camera Commissioners, and the Home Office's own Biometrics and Forensics Ethics Group.

On every occasion, government ministers have denied that new explicit legislation or regulation is needed. Indeed, as a result of a clause in the Criminal Justice Bill going through Parliament at the time of writing, the police will be able to run facial recognition searches on a database containing images of Britain's 50 million driving licence holders.[127]

The breadth of public concern around this issue, both in the UK and elsewhere, is growing clearer by the day. Cases of false arrest abound. In August 2023 in Detroit, black pregnant mother of two, Porcha Woodruff, was falsely arrested for carjacking, the third known case of an arrest made due to false facial recognition by the Detroit police department.[128]

Many cities in the US have banned the use of facial recognition, and in 2020, Microsoft, IBM, and Amazon announced that they would cease selling facial recognition technology to US law enforcement bodies.[129] In the recently agreed provisions of the EU's AI Act it now seems that a judicial process will be required to authorise its use for policing and security purposes and it will be banned in other cases. Rite Aid, a US retailer has been forbidden from deploying facial recognition technology in its stores for five years, for misidentifying people – particularly women and Black, Latino or Asian people – on 'numerous' occasions, according to a recent settlement with the Federal Trade Commission.[130]

The House of Commons Science and Technology Committee, successively in 2018 and in 2019, reiterated its conclusion that what they described as automatic facial recognition should not be deployed until concerns over the technology's effectiveness and potential bias had been fully resolved, and called on the government to issue a moratorium on the use of facial recognition technology and for no further trials to take place until a legislative framework has been introduced and guidance on trial protocols, and an oversight and evaluation system, has been established. It also called for a minister to be appointed with responsibility for making sure that the Nolan standards are observed for algorithm use in local authorities and the public sector and for departments to publicly declare where and how they use them.

The Ada Lovelace Institute, in its *Countermeasures* report[131] and the associated *Ryder Review* in June 2022, identified the need and called for new primary legislation to govern the use of biometric technologies by both public and private actors, for a new oversight body and a moratorium until comprehensive legislation has been passed.

The Minderoo Centre for Technology & Democracy in *A Sociological Audit: Assessing Police Use of Facial Recognition* in 2022[132] showed how police use of facial recognition fails to incorporate many of the known practices for the safe and ethical use of large-scale data systems, well beyond the concern of bias in facial recognition algorithms. Their results also showed a lack of proactive consultations with the public, especially marginalised communities that might be most affected by AFR deployment and it joined calls for a ban on police use of facial recognition in public spaces.

The Ada Lovelace Institute likewise has recommended that there should be a voluntary pause on the sale and use of live facial recognition technology to allow public engagement and consultation to take place. We need to put a stop to this unregulated invasion of our privacy and have a careful review so that the use can be paused while a proper regulatory framework is put in place.

Most recently Big Brother Watch's very comprehensive report *Biometric Britain*,[133] published in 2023, lays out an overwhelming case for a complete moratorium on the deployment of this technology.

They advocate that the UK should also have a root and branch surveillance camera and biometrics review which seeks to increase accountability and protect fundamental rights. The review should investigate:

- the equality and human rights implications of the use of automated facial recognition technology
- the data protection implications of the use of that technology
- the scale of surveillance we live under
- the quality and accuracy of the technology
- recommendations for addressing issues identified by the review, including the regulations and interventions needed to uphold our rights governing how biometric data is or would be processed and shared between entities involved in the use of facial recognition.

The House of Lords Justice and Home Affairs Committee is still on the case. In January 2024, its Chair, Baroness Hamwee, wrote to the UK Home Secretary after an investigation into the use of live facial recognition (LFR) technology by police forces in England and Wales.

She emphasised the Committee's findings in respect of LFR:

- The absence of a foundation in law for its deployment.
- The lack of clear standards and regulation in respect of its use.
- The importance of consistent approaches to training in its use by police forces in England and Wales.[134]

Postscript: LFR in schools

The use of facial recognition technology extends beyond policing and security. In the autumn of 2021, the news broke in the Financial Times that facial recognition software in cashless payment systems, piloted in a Gateshead school, had been adopted in nine Ayrshire schools. It was clear that this software was becoming widely adopted both sides of the border with 27 already using it in England and another 35 or so in the pipeline at the time.[135]

The supplier in question, CRB Cunninghams, attempted to reassure on the basis, as they told Sky News, that this was not a 'normal live facial recognition system … It's not recording all the time. And the operator at the till point has to physically touch the screen.'

According to North Ayrshire Council's published Data Protection Impact Assessment,[136] the source of the data for this facial recognition is a faceprint template. The facial recognition software mathematically maps an individual's facial features (such as the length and width of the nose, the distance between the eyes and the shape of the cheekbones) and stores this data as a faceprint template. It seems that the biometric profiles used as a comparison for the images of students in the queue are stored by the schools themselves, either on-premises or in a specific cloud for that school.

Its use was 'temporarily paused' by North Ayrshire council after objections from privacy campaigners and an intervention from the Information Commissioner's Office, but questions remained about use by the other schools and whether this technology would continue to be deployed in schools.

This was an extraordinary use of children's biometric data for this purpose when there were so many other alternatives available. The government response to a debate initiated by the author on the use of facial recognition in schools, in November 2021,[137] highlighted that the Department for Education's guidance needed to be updated to incorporate the latest advice from the ICO on the use of live facial recognition technology in public places and its recommendations and next steps for data controllers.

At the time of the debate, it seemed to be the case that the Department had no data on the use of biometrics in schools. There was also the question under GDPR as to whether in fact it could be used at all under data protection law, given the age groups involved, because of what is called 'the power imbalance which makes it hard to refuse'. This raises whether the pupils' or parents' consent was obtained, what information was given to them when obtaining it, and whether other methods are available which are more protective of children's data.

Without a clear understanding of the regulatory framework, it was clearly not enough for the schools in question to carry out a data protection impact assessment. The original DPIA carried out by North Ayrshire was inadequate.

In some jurisdictions – New York, France, and Sweden – its use in schools has already been banned or severely limited.[138] If there are gaps in our data protection laws, we should urgently tighten them to ensure that children under the age of 18 are comprehensively protected from facial recognition technology.

Subsequently, the Department for Education has produced *Guidance on Protection of Biometric Data of Children in Schools and Colleges* (July 2022)[139] which reminds governing bodies and headteachers and others in schools and colleges that biometric data of children is special category data and that careful consideration should be given to the purpose for its use and whether the processing is necessary and proportionate. Explicitly, the guidance says:

> *Facial recognition will often not be appropriate in schools and colleges if other options are available to achieve similar goals, like paying for school lunches. Schools and colleges must establish that facial recognition is both necessary and proportionate within the school and college environment.*

The guidance also emphasises the importance of data protection impact assessments, of the need for parental consent, for pupil and student understanding, and the offering of alternative methods of access to services.

This represents a significant victory, perhaps, in preventing the relentless onward march of live facial recognition technology at least in an educational context.

More broadly, however, the UK public sector stands at a critical moment, as the use of AI rapidly increases across different sectors in the UK, posing a range of novel challenges. Many of these AI-powered systems, like facial recognition technology, involve processing of personal data which is highly intrusive and can have very serious consequences for the individuals affected. Facial recognition surveillance poses a serious risk to the rights of the British public and threatens to transform our public spaces into ones in which people feel under the constant control of corporations and the government.

Autonomous weapons systems

Then we have the whole Defence and Lethal Autonomous Weapons Systems (LAWS) space, which in many ways is an even more concerning story.

In 2018 the House of Lords Select Committee on AI addressed the issue of military use of AI and stated that 'perhaps the most emotive and high stakes area of AI development today is its use for military purposes', recommending that this area merited a 'full inquiry on its own'.

The issue was raised again in the follow-up report *AI in the UK: No Room for Complacency* in 2020.[140] As the Committee explored the issue, it discovered that the UK's then definition, which included the phrase 'An autonomous system is capable of understanding higher-level intent and direction' was clearly out of step with the definitions used by most other governments and imposed a much higher threshold on what might be considered autonomous.

In November 2020, when the follow-up report was being written, the then Prime Minister Boris Johnson announced the creation of the Autonomy Development Centre to 'accelerate the research, development, testing, integration and deployment of world-leading artificial intelligence and autonomous systems.'[141]

As a result, the follow-up report concluded: 'We believe that the work of the Autonomy Development Centre will be inhibited by the failure to align the UK's definition of autonomous weapons with international partners: doing so must be a first priority for the Centre once established.'

LAWS were the subject of Professor Stuart Russell's Second Reith Lecture in 2021.[142] As he said, the use of AI in military applications – such as small anti-personnel weapons – is of particular concern: 'Those are the ones that are very easily scalable, meaning you could put a million of them in a single truck and you could open the back and off they go and wipe out a whole city.'

During its inquiry the Committee discovered that there was, at the time, not even a definition in use by NATO or the UK of an autonomous or automated system. That has changed as the UK has now accepted NATO's definitions of '*autonomous*' and '*autonomy*', which are now in working use within the Alliance. As the UK Ministry of Defence (MOD) emphasised, these definitions refer to broad categories of autonomous systems, and not specifically to LAWS.

So, despite accepting the NATO definition of '*automated system*' and '*autonomous system*', the MOD did not (and still does not) have an operative definition of lethal autonomous weapon systems. Given that the most problematic aspect – autonomy – has been defined, that is an extraordinary state of affairs.

It seems that the term LAWS itself is not used consistently: some parties use it to refer to weapon systems that operate without meaningful human control; others use it to refer to weapons that operate with some degree of autonomy. The definition of such a system is therefore both technically complicated and highly subjective. The MOD does not have an operative definition of LAWS and there is similarly no international agreement on the definition or characteristics of LAWS.

This allowed the government to assert that the UK does not possess fully autonomous weapon systems and has no intention of developing them. Such systems are not yet in existence and are not likely to be for many years, if at all.

As a result, a great number of questions arise about liability and accountability, particularly in international humanitarian law, and the very real fear is that autonomous weapons will undermine these international laws of war.

There are particular risks posed by these weapons. For instance:

- **Sufficiency of technology**: Whether AI technology can accurately identify and target threats is a fundamental question. Current AI systems are highly brittle and struggle to generalise or adapt to conditions outside of a narrow range of assumptions.
- **Escalation and proliferation**: Removing humans from the battlefield may reduce hesitancy to use force and thus escalate conflicts. The increased speed of autonomous systems, as well as any unintended behaviour, could risk inadvertent escalation and heighten crisis instability.

- **Accountability**: There is a lack of clarity about who, if anyone, is responsible for the actions of an autonomous system if it behaves unlawfully or not as intended.
- **Cyber security**: Making use of systems underpinned by computer software leaves them vulnerable to cyber-attack. Attackers could seek to take control of a system, disrupt operations, gather confidential information or tamper with the training data.

There are fine words in the subsequent UK Integrated Review of 2021 *Global Britain in a Competitive Age*[143] that the 'UK remains at the forefront of the rapidly evolving debate on responsible development and use of AI and Autonomy, working with liberal–democratic partners to shape international legal, ethical and regulatory norms and standards.' Despite this and despite support across the UK political spectrum and from nearly 70 states and thousands of scientists at meetings of the Convention on Conventional Weapons (CCW) the UK government has to date not supported moves to limit the use of LAWS.[144]

Development of AI is clearly a priority for the military. General Sir Mark Carleton-Smith, the former Chief of the General Staff said that he foresaw the army of the future as '*the integration of boots and bots*'.[145] The UK government announced in March 2021 that it would be spending at least £6.6bn in military Research and Development (R&D) over the next four years. This spending would support the development of 'next generation' weapons, with the Royal Air Force receiving more than £2bn for the Future Combat Air System, which will 'deliver an innovative mix of crewed, uncrewed and autonomous platforms including swarming drones'.

As part of the Defence Review in 2020, former Prime Minister Boris Johnson said that the UK would invest another £1.5bn in military research and development designed to master the new technologies of warfare, and establish a new Defence Centre for AI.[146]

A recent UK Campaign to Stop Killer Robots report has suggested that the UK research sector has insufficient safeguards to minimise the risks that government-funded research will not be misused and incorporate or help facilitate the production of LAWS.[147]

The UK's Defence AI strategy released in June 2022[148] recognised that there is a line that should not be crossed in terms of machines making decisions in combat. However, the position provides no indications of where this line is to be drawn. The strategy was produced without any public consultation. Together with its lack of detail, it seems the public and parliamentarians are being told by the government and its military, 'leave it to us' to determine what is appropriate.

The government, however, have not yet explained how legal and ethical frameworks and support for personnel engaged in operations will also change as a consequence of the use of new technologies, particularly autonomous weapons, which could be deployed by our armed forces or our allies. This is all the more so in a multinational context where other countries may be using technology which either we would not deploy, or the use of which could create potential vulnerabilities for our troops.

Defence ministers continually denied that they use systems that 'employ lethal force without context-appropriate human involvement'. But this, as the UK-UNA have pointed out, is a step further than the original position that the UK *does not possess fully autonomous weapon systems and has no intention of developing them*.

In reply to oral questions in the Lords, Defence Minister Baroness Goldie said, *'The UK and our partners are unconvinced by the calls for a further binding instrument. International humanitarian law provides a robust principle-based framework for the regulation of weapons deployment and use. A focus on effects is most effective in dealing with complex systems in conflict.'* [149]

And further, 'It is not possible to transfer accountability to a machine. Human responsibility for the use of a system to achieve an effect cannot be removed, irrespective of the level of autonomy in that system or the use of enabling technologies such as AI.'

But new technologies are changing how military operations are conducted. As we know drone warfare is already a fact of life – possibly autonomous Turkish drones may have been deployed in Libya and Syria, and likewise Iranian drones in Ukraine.[150]

The UN Secretary General, António Guterres has been quoted earlier as saying that autonomous machines with the power and discretion to select targets and take lives without human involvement are politically unacceptable, morally repugnant, and should be prohibited by international law. Yet we still have no international limitation agreement.

From the UK government perspective that seems to have implied that there will always be a human in the loop and there will never be a fully autonomous weapon deployed. If the legal duties are to remain the same for our Armed Forces, these weapons must surely at all times remain under human control and there will never be autonomous deployment.

The Artificial Intelligence Strategy for NATO published in October 2021 set out six principles:[151]

Lawfulness: AI applications will be developed and used in accordance with national and international law, including international humanitarian law and human rights law, as applicable.

Responsibility and accountability: AI applications will be developed and used with appropriate levels of judgment and care; clear human responsibility shall apply in order to ensure accountability.

Explainability and traceability: AI applications will be appropriately understandable and transparent, including through the use of review methodologies, sources, and procedures. This includes verification, assessment, and validation mechanisms at either a NATO and/or national level.

Reliability: AI applications will have explicit, well-defined use cases. The safety, security, and robustness of such capabilities will be subject to testing and assurance within those use cases across their entire life cycle, including through established NATO and/or national certification procedures.

Governability: AI applications will be developed and used according to their intended functions and will allow for: appropriate human–machine interaction; the ability to detect and avoid unintended consequences; and the ability to take steps, such as disengagement or deactivation of systems, when such systems demonstrate unintended behaviour.

Bias mitigation: Proactive steps will be taken to minimise any unintended bias in the development and use of AI applications and in data sets.

This was followed in June 2022 by the UK Ministry of Defence (MOD) paper *Ambitious, Safe, Responsible: Our approach to the delivery of AI-enabled capability in Defence* as part of the UK AI Defence Strategy.[152]

This had a rather different emphasis to the NATO principles: The UK aspires to exploit AI comprehensively, accelerating 'best in class' AI-enabled capabilities into service in order to make all parts of Defence significantly more efficient and effective. The emphasis is on Safety, Legality – in accordance with the body of applicable UK and international law, ethics (setting up of a largely internal Ethics Advisory Panel) with a slightly different five principles:

- Human centricity
- Responsibility
- Understanding
- Bias and harm mitigation
- Reliability

The UK government clearly considers that the provisions of international law – particularly International Humanitarian Law (IHL) – and the existing regulatory frameworks which apply to the development of weapons systems in Defence are appropriate to govern emerging technologies in this area. It also clearly believes that it is taking an active role as moral and ethical leader on the global stage and that we are aligned with our key allies.

Professor Stuart Russell, in his 2021 Reith lectures mentioned earlier, however, said, '*The inevitable endpoint is that autonomous weapons become cheap, selective weapons of mass destruction. Clearly, this would be a disaster for international security.*'

This was clearly unfinished business and needed further examination. In company with a former Secretary of State for Defence and a former Chief of Defence Staff, the author argued for a special inquiry to be held into how legal and ethical frameworks need to be updated in response to novel defence technologies. As a result, a new House of Lords Select Committee was appointed to explore a number of key areas related to LAWS such as:

- What is a truly autonomous weapon?
- What is technologically feasible at present?
- What scenarios for their use can we envisage?
- What are the risks of their permitted use and of their escalation, especially to our populations?
- Should we be outsourcing our defence to AI and algorithms?
- What moral and ethical principles apply?
- Should there always be a human in control? What is meaningful control?
- How does the use of autonomous weapon systems conflict with our civil aspirations for the development of ethical AI?
- What legal principles already apply or should apply? Where do they fit within current UK and NATO defence policy and strategy?
- Should an international limitation/proliferation agreement be reached similar to nuclear and biological weapons?

The Committee produced its report in December 2023. *Proceed with Caution: Artificial Intelligence in Weapons Systems.*[153]

The Committee was likewise surprised that the UK government does not currently have an operational definition of AWS and indeed suggested its own:

'Fully' autonomous weapon systems: Systems that, once activated, can identify, select, and engage targets with lethal force without further intervention by an operator.

'Partially' autonomous weapon systems: Systems featuring varying degrees of decision-making autonomy in critical functions such as identification, classification, interception and engagement.

It was somewhat sceptical of MOD policy in this area and concluded that the government's aspiration of being 'ambitious, safe, and responsible' had not lived up to reality and must be translated into practical implementation.

In doing so, it concluded that the government must seek, establish, and retain public confidence and democratic endorsement in the development and use of AI generally, and especially in respect of AWS. Crucial to this process will be that the government should lead by example in international engagement on regulation of AWS. A key element in this will be prohibiting the use of AI in nuclear command, control, and communications. The government should adopt an operational definition of AWS, ensure human control at all stages of an AWS's lifecycle, and that its procurement processes are appropriately designed for the world of AI.

We are still a long way away from reaching international consensus on limitation of AWS or agreement on how it can be deployed, but shortly before the report's publication, on 1st November 2023, we saw what many considered to be the historic move: the first-ever UN resolution on autonomous weapons was adopted at the UN General Assembly in New York with support from the UK.[154]

The resolution affirms that international law, in particular the Charter of the United Nations, international humanitarian law, and international human rights law, applies to autonomous weapons systems and begins the process of consulting states and NGOs and 'the scientific community and industry' on autonomous weapons systems. The provisional agenda of the 2024 United Nations General Assembly will include an item entitled, 'Lethal autonomous weapons systems' – providing a further platform within UN fora for states to pursue action to address this issue.

Beyond this resolution the UK government has been urged by a large number of human rights organisations[155] to commit to making urgent progress towards establishing a new international law on autonomous weapons systems outside of the deadlocked Convention on Certain Conventional Weapons and play an active and meaningful role in advancing negotiation. Given the UK's support for the resolution in the first Committee in November the author likewise urges the UK government to take these next steps in playing a leadership role.

Let us hope for, and work for, further progress in the coming months and years.

5 AI and IP Rewarding Human Creativity

With the advent of generative AI systems, there has been an increasing debate about intellectual property rights and ownership, with their ability to deliver creative artefacts such as literature, art, and music, especially where it is in the style of an established artist or writer. Potential use of AI by film studios to synthesise performance and emulate writing was at the root of the recently settled writers' and actors' strike in the US.

IP in training material

AI developers – particularly now the creators of large language models – rely on high-quality data and content to develop reliable and innovative AI-driven applications. By the same token, content and data-driven businesses themselves have seen a rapid increase in the use of AI technology and machine-learning, either for news summaries, data gathering efforts, translations for research and journalistic purposes, or to assist organisations to save time by processing large amounts of text and other data at scale and speed.

Digital technologies, including AI, are – and will continue to be – of critical importance to these industries, helping create content, new products, and value-added services to deliver to a broad range of corporate and retail clients. Whether in news media or cross-industry research, publishers are themselves investing in AI; continued collaboration with start-ups and academia is creating tailored materials for wide populations of beneficiaries (students, academia, research organisations, and even marketers of consumer publishing products).

It is of paramount importance to balance the needs of future AI development with the legal, commercial and economic rights of data and content owners and the need to incentivise new AI adoption with recognition of the rights of existing content owners.

In 2020, the *Guardian* newspaper published an op-ed headed: 'A robot wrote this entire article. Are you scared yet, human?'[156] This was written by a natural language processing system, Open AI's GPT-3. Very convincingly it urged humans to be 'careful about the evolution of artificial intelligence'.

Although these large language models have been talked about as a competitor to, or replacement for, search engines, there are huge doubts about the accuracy of these models which make up academic references, news items, and even legal precedents – they 'hallucinate' in the phrase that has come to be adopted about them.

Capabilities for image creation have grown equally rapidly. In 2018 a portrait of Edmond de Belamy, created by a collaboration between an art collective called Obvious and a generative adversarial network (GAN) algorithm sold for nearly half a million dollars at Christie's.[157] Ai-Da, a life-size AI robot visual artist which appeared before an inquiry into the future of the creative industries by the House of Lords Communications and Digital Committee has been mentioned earlier.[158] In 2023, German artist Boris Eldagsen won a Sony world photography award with an AI-generated image and then refused to take the prize.[159]

In 2022, Open AI's ChatGPT and GPT-4, the latest evolutions of the GPT family, were launched. They are even more sophisticated. Not only can they write articles virtually indistinguishable from human-created pieces but it seems they can pass some serious law exams and compete in the Biology Olympiad. Since ChatGPT's release, OpenAI has revamped the language model by giving it new image generation capabilities via DALL-E 3, access to real-time information through Bing – the Microsoft search engine – and also new voice and image capabilities via GPT-4V, or GPT-4 Vision. Some consider that this type of multimodal model is paving the way towards Artificial General Intelligence, or at least giving the impression of doing so.

Since the launch of generative AI platforms, such as ChatGPT-4, DALL.E 2, and Stable Diffusion, there has been an increasing realisation of their potential impact on human creativity, both positive and negative. There are clearly great opportunities in relation to the use of AI, and many sectors are already using the technology in a variety of different ways to enhance their creativity and make it easier for the public to discover new content.

But as well as being now widely understood as a tool for widespread assistance with written work and image creation there has been the dawning realisation that these generative tools have in most cases been trained on content in such a way that the intellectual property rights of human creators have been infringed.

This presents challenges and questions over authorship and intellectual property rights, and many artists and writers feel threatened. There is an increasing debate about intellectual property rights and ownership with AI delivering creative artefacts such as literature, art, and music, especially where it is in the style of an established artist or writer. The recent strikes in Hollywood by the Writers Guild of America (WGA) and by the Screen Actors Guild-American Federation of Television and Radio Artists (SAG-AFTRA) were both prompted specifically by the threat of AI and were settled on terms which specifically deal with the use by studios in the form of the Alliance of Motion Picture and Television Producers of AI systems in relation to their output.[160]

As regards material used to train generative AI systems, the most contested aspect is copyright. This is the exclusive right to make copies of a work; the ability to prepare derivative works; the right to distribute copies of the work to the public; and the right to perform or display the work publicly. This means that if the training process requires copies to be made from a dataset containing copyright works, the rights of the holders of the data used in these processes may be infringed. In addition, if the AI system has been trained using a dataset containing copyright works, there is also the potential risk that the output produced by that AI system will materially resemble, or completely reproduce, parts of those copyright works, therefore potentially infringing the rightsholder's right to make derivative works.

In Chapter 8 a contrast will be made between the UK and EU regulatory regime, with an observation that the EU is adopting a stricter mandatory approach to regulation and the adoption of standards. In the case of intellectual property rights and AI, however, the EU seems to be adopting a more permissive approach.

Representatives of the European Parliament, EU Member States, and

European Commission reached a provisional agreement on the EU AI Act (the AIA) in December 2023. Only in June 2023, 14 months after the bill was first introduced did EU legislators consider it necessary to seek to include specific obligations in relation to foundation models used in AI systems intended to generate content. This has been one of the main areas of debate between the EU legislators.

At the time of writing it seems that providers of foundation models will have to draw up and maintain technical documentation of the model including its training and testing processes and the results of its evaluation when seeking to reproduce copyright works and draw up and make publicly available a sufficiently detailed summary about the content used for training of the foundation model, according to a template provided by the AI Office.

That is the positive aspect and one the UK could and should follow but alongside that, creators and/or trainers of generative AI platforms may be able to take advantage of the text and data mining exception (TDM) in Article 4 of the EU Digital Single Market Copyright Directive. Unless the rightsholder has opted out, the activity of reproducing copyright-protected materials for the purposes of training the AI would typically be covered.[161]

The rightsholder, however, is entitled to reserve its rights through what are called 'appropriate means' such as using machine-readable means, like metadata or terms and conditions. Where the rights have been expressly reserved by way of an opt-out, providers of foundation models will need to obtain an authorisation from rightsholders if they want to carry out text and data mining over such works.

This obviously presents a great risk to rightsholders if they are not aware of the Article 4 TDM and fail to expressly opt out.

Other countries such as Japan and Singapore also have broad exceptions and, depending on the facts, TDM may also be fair use under US law.

In July 2023, the Authors Coalition, a coalition of US creative workers and other writers, illustrators, photographers, graphic artists, digital media workers, journalists, novelists, playwrights, composers, and songwriters, issued a joint statement urging EU legislators to promptly cure what they considered to be violations of the Berne Convention. They also urged the

US government to use all available means to bring the EU in compliance with Berne:

> *Much of the copying of our works for generative AI, including 'scraping' of Web pages and compilation of 'datasets' for use in generative AI, has been carried out from, and/or by entities in, the European Union, claiming to rely on the exceptions to copyright for 'text and data mining' (TDM) in Articles 3 and 4 of the Directive on Copyright in the Digital Single Market ('DSM Directive') enacted by the European Union in 2019.*

> *But allowing these exceptions to be applied to copying for ingestion and reuse by generative AI systems constitutes a significant violation of the obligations of EU member states as parties to the Berne Convention ... We urge the European Union to promptly cure this violation of the Berne Convention and provide effective redress for the violations which have already occurred.*[162]

UK law, however, does not have a text and data mining exemption of this width, as the implementation deadline for the Directive which contained the EU's exemption occurred after the expiry of the UK/EU Brexit transition period. The exception is limited to AI training for non-commercial research purposes, and publishers owning content subject to copyright have developed a strong licensing regime for the use of copyright material.

In June 2022, the UK IPO published a response to its consultation which was intended to seek 'evidence and views on a range of options on how AI should be dealt with in the patent and copyright systems'. In the response, the UK IPO indicated that it planned to greatly broaden the UK's text and data mining exception to allow text and data mining for any purpose (including a commercial one) and without any ability for rightsholders to opt out. These proposals drew widespread criticism from across the creative industries and rightsholder groups on the basis that the current licensing regime was fit for purpose.[163]

In February 2023, in the face of a backlash from the music industry and other creative sectors, and thanks to the then IP Minister George Freeman

MP being persuaded by among others the Alliance for Intellectual Property and members of the All-Party Group on Intellectual Property, these plans were dropped.[164] The following month following recommendations made by Sir Patrick Vallance, the UK government's former Chief Scientific Advisor, in his *Pro-innovation Regulation of Technology Review*, the government nevertheless accepted that there remained a need to clarify how AI providers and users can utilise copyright works and data in order to promote AI.[165]

As a result, the UK's Intellectual Property Office is now working with users and rightsholders to assist in developing a code of practice on copyright and AI which explicitly states that its aim is to:

make licences for data mining more available. It will help to overcome barriers that AI firms and users currently face, and ensure there are protections for rightsholders. This ensures that the UK copyright framework promotes and rewards investment in creativity. It also supports the ambition for the UK to be a world leader in research and AI innovation.

It is currently envisaged that it will be entered into on a voluntary basis.

The issue of copyright infringement by AI developers is set to continue to cause controversy. In recent months, Getty Images has indicated its objection to the use of its copyright works by generative AI and has initiated court proceedings in the US and the UK against Stability AI, a generative AI platform which creates artwork based on text instructions input by users.[166] Getty has claimed in a statement on its website that Stability AI has:

unlawfully copied and processed millions of images protected by copyright and the associated metadata owned or represented by Getty Images absent a licence to benefit Stability AI's commercial interests and to the detriment of the content creators.

The New York Times has recently filed a lawsuit against Microsoft and OpenAI, the company behind ChatGPT, accusing them of copyright infringement and abusing the newspaper's intellectual property.[167] The Times accused Microsoft and OpenAI of creating a business model based on 'mass copyright infringement', stating their AI systems 'exploit and, in many cases, retain large portions of the copyrightable expression contained in those works'. In its court filing, the publisher said it seeks to hold Microsoft and OpenAI to account for 'billions of dollars in statutory and actual damages' it believes that it is owed for 'unlawful copying and use of *The Times*'s uniquely valuable works'.

All these cases will raise interesting issues as to whether and when the use of copyright works to train AI systems will infringe copyright, and as to whether any defences may apply.

Can AI create a copyrighted work?

A lawyer colleague of the author's recently asked themselves the question: *Can a robot write a symphony?* And answered: *With a rapidly growing armoury of AI tools, the answer is 'highly likely'*.

A more problematic question is whether it and any other AI-created works can attract copyright protection. Given the increased creative output of AI, there are some fundamental issues regarding AI and IP raised by intellectual property experts such as Francis Gurry, the former Head of WIPO.[168] These include:

> **Originality**. Do we require different standards for machines?
> **Authorship/inventorship**. Is there a distinction between human and machine authors and attributing higher value and longer protection to the former?
> **Reward**: Do we need to reward an AI for creativity?
> **Ownership**: Who has ownership of the IP created?

As Francis Gurry has said,

> *The fundamental goals of the IP system have always been to encourage new technologies and creative works, and to create a sustainable economic basis for invention and creation.*

But is it just about economics? Should we be making more of copyright and moral rights for human-created works?

The situation in the EU is relatively clear. Although there is no formal definition of 'author' in EU legal texts, case law of the Court of Justice of the EU establishes that only a human can be considered an author of copyrightable works.

The position under UK law is more positive. In the UK we already do in essence make a distinction between human creativity and true copyright which protects a literary, dramatic, musical, or artistic work where the author is specified as the person who creates it and, on the other hand, what are called 'related rights', which includes sound recordings and films, and broadcast rights where the rights granted are essentially in return for investment.

Section 9 (3) of the UK's Copyright, Designs and Patents Act 1988 (CDPA)[169] has an existing solution. This provides protection for computer-generated literary, dramatic, musical, or artistic works. The UK is one of only a handful of countries to protect works generated by a computer where there is no human creator. The 'author' of a 'computer-generated work' is defined as 'the person by whom the arrangements necessary for the creation of the work are undertaken'. Protection lasts for 50 years from the date the work is made.

Consequently, the owner of the literary work and the copyright subsisting in it, if it were original, would be, alternatively:

a) the operator of an AI system (aligning its inputs and selecting its datasets and data fields); or

b) their employer, if employed; or

c) a third party, if the operator has a contract assigning such rights outside of employment context.

To be original, a work must be an author's or artist's own intellectual creation, reflecting their personality.

At the other end of the scale, a human who simply provides training data to an AI system and presses 'analyse' is unlikely to be considered the author of the resulting work. In this way we believe that the existing copyright legislative framework under the UK's current copyright law adequately addresses the current needs of AI developers. New entrants and disruptors can, in our opinion, work within the existing framework which adequately caters for the existing and foreseeable future.

The question of copyright protection for AI-generated works is therefore to some extent debatable due to the varying degree of human involvement required for an AI tool to produce creative works, and the nuanced interpretations that could be applied to the concepts of 'originality' and 'creativity'.

Arguably, the person making the arrangements could be seen as the owner or user of any AI platform used to make an artwork. But the situation becomes less clear when seeking to establish whether the work is sufficiently original to benefit from copyright protection when using generative software. It is uncertain to what extent a user would need to interact with a generative AI program in order to have demonstrated sufficient originality.

In the author's view, in these circumstances there is a case for reduction in the term of rights for a work created under 9(3) from 50 to 5 or 10 years and for the person making the arrangements to be treated as the operator (that is, the person that guides the AI to apply certain data or parameters and shapes the outcome) not the owner of the AI system. AI systems already have access to content from global providers and create derivative content (whether under licence or not) and do so at great speed with little or no investment or 'sweat of the brow'. It can therefore be argued that in fact the level of protection should be reduced to be proportionate to the time, effort, and investment involved.

Copyright law does, however, need to be clarified to ensure that it is the operator or his/her employer of the AI system – that is, the person that guides the AI system to apply certain data or parameters and shapes the outcome – that is the copyright owner, and not the owner of the AI system.

Apart from that, there is in our view there is no particular evidence that the existing UK copyright legislative framework fails to adequately address the current needs of AI developers or that current copyright law creates an undue disparity between the interests of AI developers and investors and content owners. The existing copyright regime under current UK legislation, the CDPA, in our view reflects a balance that fairly protects those investing in data creation without giving an unfair advantage to technology companies offering AI-enabled content creation services.

Responsible AI developers should seek to license content. It is important that AI developers making copies – whether of text, music, images, or other creative content, recognise that they will be infringing copyright and that the ingestion of content requires permission from rightsholders.

If the content owners of underlying data materials withhold the licensing of, or access to, such materials or attempt to price them at a level that is unfair, the answer is for competition remedies to be invoked via the competition regulators. We deal in more detail with that aspect in Chapter 8.

US Copyright and AI

US copyright law differs considerably from the UK position. The US Copyright Office recognises copyright only in works 'created by a human being'. Courts have likewise declined to extend copyright protection to non-human authors. There is its famous decision, for example, that a monkey which took a series of photos lacked standing to sue under the Copyright Act.

In February 2023, the US Copyright Office (USCO) issued a decision[170] on artwork created by the generative AI, Midjourney, in which images are created by feeding the program a series of text prompts. In their letter to the author of the book for which the images were produced, the USCO stated that the images were not eligible to be protected by a copyright registration on the basis that the artworks which were generated by AI 'are not the product of human authorship'.

However, in a recent policy statement in March 2023,[171] the USCO stated that works partially created by generative AI may in fact be eligible for copyright protections. The guidelines state that individuals applying for works with AI content can in fact claim copyright protection for their own contributions to the work. For example, a visual artist can claim sole authorship but must add a disclaimer that the selection, coordination, and arrangement of x-amount of content is of the artist themselves, and that y-amount of the work was generated by artificial intelligence.

The US Copyright Office, in August 2023, however, issued a comprehensive notice of inquiry and request for public comment to inform its new 'study of the copyright law and policy issues raised by artificial intelligence (AI)'.[172] The request includes dozens of questions, and the issues in it broadly include (1) transparency, licensing, and fair use considerations for use of copyrighted works to train AI models; (2) copyrightability of AI-generated outputs; (3) whether AI models and output may infringe copyright and/or protections for copyright management information; and (4) whether a federal right of publicity law or other protections should be put in place to prohibit unauthorised creation of AI-generated outputs that imitate the style of a human creator. Given the rise of AI-related IP litigation in the US it is notable that the new AI study seems to have a real sense of urgency, with a report to Congress with policy recommendations due by the end of 2024. This may well lead to radical changes to US copyright law.

Patents and AI

Professor Ryan Abbott, author of the *Reasonable Robot: Artificial Intelligence and the Law* (CUP 2020), is a leading academic and practitioner as regards AI inventorship for patents. As a practitioner, he has been most famously advancing a test case internationally on whether an invention generated by an AI called 'DABUS', created by computer scientist Dr Stephen Thaler, but without a traditional human inventor, can receive patent protection.

This case in the UK, Thaler v Comptroller-General of Patents, Trade Marks and Designs[173] has helped provide guidance for the UK's AI industry, and it has stimulated discussion about how intellectual property law should respond to advances in technology. We are not adherents to his belief that an AI should be treated as the inventor, but the debate is an important one as jurisdictions such as the UK choose how to drive forward the governance of AI systems.

A critical feature of this case and the applicant's corresponding cases elsewhere – including the US – is the absence of a human inventor; the applicant claimed that the inventor was DABUS and DABUS alone. So, this decision does not mean that inventions developed by humans using AI as a tool cannot be patented under UK law if they meet the statutory patentability requirements and name a human inventor.

Authoritative guidance on how AI-created inventions fit into this scheme, where no human inventor is mentioned, is given in the decision in *Thaler* in the UK's Appeals Court. All three judges in *Thaler* agreed that under the UK Patents Act (PA) 1977[174] an inventor must be a person, and as a machine is not a person it, therefore, cannot be an 'inventor' for the purposes of section 7(2) of the Act.

In December 2023, the UK Supreme Court[175] confirmed the judgement of the Court of Appeal that a patent requires disclosure of an inventor, and that under the existing scheme an inventor must be a natural person, and so in the case of an AI-generated invention without an identifiable human inventor the invention is inherently unprotectable.

Lord Kitchin, in his Supreme Court judgement said:

Whether or not thinking machines were capable of devising inventions in 1977, it is clear to me that Parliament did not have them in mind when enacting this scheme. If patents are to be granted in respect of inventions made by machines, the 1977 Act will have to be amended.

In the Court of Appeal, Lord Justice Birss dissented on the crucial point whether it was an impediment to the grant of an application that the creator of an invention was a machine, as such. He stated that it was simply that a machine inventor cannot be treated as an inventor for the purpose of granting the application. In the author's view, in principle, Lord Justice Birss's approach was the right one. There should therefore be no need for the patent system to identify AI as the inventor or to create entirely new rights. Inventions created by AI, or with the assistance of AI, should be patentable.

In copyright law the author and first owner of any AI-assisted or -created work will be the person who creates the work, or their employer if that person is an employee or a third party if the operator has a contract assigning such rights outside of employment context. As the emphasis in copyright law suggests, creating a 'work' is in essence a human activity. Similar principles should apply to patents as with copyright. In addition, as with AI creations for copyright purposes, the key is the operation and control of the machine/AI producing the invention, not ownership of the AI itself.

There are signs however that UK patent law is moving in this direction. A recent decision from the UK High Court (*Emotional Perception AI Ltd v Comptroller-General of Patents* [2023] EWHC 2948 (Ch)) decided that the use of an aspect of Artificial Intelligence, namely an Artificial Neural Network (ANN), on the facts of this case, did not fall foul of the statutory exclusion from patentability of 'a program for a computer … as such'. This decision may well pave the way to make it easier to patent AI inventions in the UK.

It should also be said that, in the US, the Patent and Trademark Office refused to issue patents for DABUS's invention and appeals, including to the US Supreme Court in 2023, have been unsuccessful on similar grounds, that patents can be issued only to human inventors.[176] The Legal Board of Appeal of the European Patent Office (EPO) ruled similarly in December 2021 and confirmed the EPO's decision that an inventor in a patent application must be a human being under the European Patent Convention (EPC).[177]

Performing rights and AI

Then there are the issues relating to performing rights: the copying of actors', musicians', artists', and other creators' images, voices, likenesses, styles, and attributes by AI systems. The all-important aspect of human and machine interface heavily impacts creative performers and artists. The use of AI has grown rapidly across the audio and entertainment industry in recent years, from automated audio books and voice assistants to deepfake videos and text-to-speech tools.

AI-made 'performance synthetisation' is one of the ways that the technology is used in the entertainment industry. This is the process of creating a performance by manipulating the likeness of a performance or a performer. Examples include deepfake videos in which a person in an existing image or video is replaced with someone else's likeness.

But in the view of many, IP law has failed to keep pace. And this is leading to performers being exploited. AI is being used to clone performers' voices and likenesses. Performers are having their image, voice or likeness reproduced by others, using AI technology, without their consent.

Because of loopholes in the law, performers are not being fairly paid for the reproduction of their work – and sometimes not paid at all. In an Equity survey in 2022, 79% of performers who have undertaken AI work felt they did not have a full understanding of their performers' rights before signing the contract. And 65% of performers thought that the development of AI technology poses a threat to employment opportunities in the performing arts sector.[178]

As mentioned earlier, the threat from AI was at the root of the recent Hollywood actors' strike and the Stop AI Stealing the Show campaign in the UK by Equity, the actors' union in the UK. It is important that creators and artists derive the full benefit of technology such as AI-made performance synthetisation and streaming and that artists' names, voices, images, and likenesses are sufficiently protected. AI could have a hugely positive impact on the entertainment industry, but we need to make sure that it works for performers and not just the production companies.

Equity, in their Stop AI Stealing the Show campaign,[179] have called for the UK government to modernise the law and strengthen rights for creatives and performers. What is needed now is an independent review to explore the merits of introducing image rights and publicity rights, and ensure that the purpose of copyright in stimulating and sustaining creativity is met. Canadian voiceover artist Bev Standing is at the forefront of the campaign. She won a settlement after she sued TikTok, saying the company had used her voice for their text-to-speech feature without her permission, based on recordings she had provided for another company years earlier.[180]

In the meantime, the UK and other governments should ratify the Beijing Treaty[181] on audiovisual performances at the earliest opportunity. This would at least grant performers the right to be identified as the performer, and the right to object to any distortion, mutilation, or other modification to the recorded or broadcast material that would be prejudicial to their reputation.

The future of AI and IP

At the end of the day, AI raises the fundamental question of how the benefit and reward for IP creation is distributed. If AI can create huge quantities of IP autonomously who gets the benefit? Large corporates which have access to vast quantities of data to train their algorithms? Or should our competition regulators intrude on IP creation and dataset monopolies in a way that they have never done before? The Digital Markets Unit of the Competition and Markets Authority now being created in the UK may well need to wrestle with this.

Intellectual property regulators and policymakers too will need to keep an active watching brief. Changes to copyright laws in one country that make it more attractive for AI developers to base their operations in those locations so that text and data mining activities become more easily performed or permitted could lead to a race to the bottom – to the detriment of human creativity. International alignment on the nature of copyright and performer protection and the shape of any reform is vital. Given the global adoption of AI technology, it is also clear that an internationally harmonised approach to the protection and recognition accorded to AI-generated inventions and works is needed.

6 Digital Skills, Digital Literacy, Digital Exclusion, and the Future of Work

The digital future

Of necessity this chapter is heavily focused on the UK but it is clear that the problems discussed below are a matter of global concern.

For AI to truly be our servant and not our master it is important that our citizens have the digital skills and understanding they need to use new technologies and have access to the digital infrastructure needed to benefit from it. We need to recognise that digital and cyber skills are needed to empower individuals and organisations in the age of AI to the fullest extent.

The COVID-19 pandemic and subsequent developments in large language models has thrown the issue of digital skills and exclusion into sharp relief. AI is becoming embedded in everything we do. In particular AI will have significant implications for the ways in which society lives and works and will accelerate the disruption in the jobs market. This means that, in terms of education, skills, and reskilling, we must ensure that we are prepared for future automation of many jobs. Whatever the scale of disruption, retraining will be a lifelong necessity.

Digital skills for the future

The adoption of AI will not necessarily make huge numbers of people redundant, but as the COVID-19 pandemic is receding into the past and government has to address its economic impact, the nature of work will change and there will be a need for different jobs and skills. The adoption of AI in the private sector and government is already requiring new skills, and governments and industry must be ready to ensure that training and retraining opportunities take account of this.

As the All-Party Parliamentary Group on Digital Skills (APPGDS) in its report *Better Connected – Digital Britain by 2030* in March 2023 noted, the impact of the pandemic has further driven a shift in working pattern and mindsets, increasing the number of employees working remotely.[182] The Office for National Statistics found, for example, that the UK saw an increase of 19.6% in remote work from December 2019 to March 2022.

AI will accelerate the digital disruption in the jobs market. Many jobs will be enhanced by AI, many will disappear, and many new, as yet unknown, jobs will be created. AI will have significant implications for the ways in which society lives and works.

As long ago as 2013, Carl Benedikt Frey and Michael Osborne of the Oxford Martin School at the University of Oxford published a paper entitled *'The Future of Employment: How Susceptible Are Jobs to Computerisation?'*,[183] estimating that 47% of US jobs were at risk of automation, and management consultancy firm McKinsey in 2017 put the figure at 50%.[184] In 2018, Andy Haldane, then the Bank of England's Chief Economist, agreed.[185]

Others came to different conclusions. In particular, one study published by a group of researchers at the University of Mannheim, also in 2017,[186] suggested that only 9% of jobs were exposed to automation. The following year a study by the OECD suggested that it was actually 14%, with a further 32% of jobs not being lost as such but having a risk of 50–70%, pointing to the possibility of a significant change in the way these jobs are carried out as a result of automation. This points to changes within jobs being as significant as changes in jobs themselves.

Frey and Osborne commented some years later:

> Our estimates have often been taken to imply an employment apocalypse. Yet that is not what we intended or suggested. All we showed is that the potential scope of automation is vast, just as it was at the eve of the Second Industrial Revolution, before electricity and the internal combustion engine rendered many of the jobs that existed in 1900 redundant.[187]

Michael Osborne's 2017 paper *The Future of Skills: Employment in 2030*[188] looked at the prospects in a different way. It forecast that one in ten people are highly likely to experience a rise in demand for their job. The remaining workers are in jobs where there is greater uncertainty about the future:

these workers can boost their prospects if they can invest in the right skills. Their findings dug deeper into how we can take action to help more people prepare for the future, and they concluded:

This means that roughly seven in ten people are currently in jobs where we simply cannot know for certain what will happen. However, our findings about skills suggest that occupation redesign coupled with workforce retraining could promote growth in these occupations....

The bottom line of our research: we can all stop agonizing about machines taking our jobs. The future will be about leveraging both human and machine capabilities, and this research provides a blueprint for how we might reform education to meet the demands of the future head on.

That is the lesson the author believes we need to take from the AI employment studies to date.

A good example of current and future impact is on professional occupations. We have seen considerable impact already on the professions: lawyers are using it for due diligence and detection of anti-competitive behaviour, architects, engineers and accountants too. But so far none of this has radically changed the professional advisory model.

Far more radical changes are on the way. It is likely the machines will be able to do almost all routine professional work. As Professor Richard Susskind has long predicted, major changes in the professions are occurring as a result of AI.[189] Processing of data with the necessary algorithms will give rise to alternative ways of delivering practical professional expertise. In healthcare, the Royal Society report *Machine Learning* in 2017[190] opined that healthcare was where the biggest impact would be.

At that time it was already clear that medical imaging, and supporting administrative roles, were key areas for adoption. Fast forward five years and we now have large language models such as Med-PaLM developed by Google research which are designed to provide high-quality answers to medical questions. Just around the corner, it seems, could be multimodal foundation models for generalist medical use that are trained on massive, diverse datasets and which will be able to perform a very wide range of tasks based on a broad range of data such as images, electronic health records, laboratory results, genomics, graphs, or medical text and which can communicate directly with patients.

A key factor here is the potential hollowing out of professional skills. How are young professionals and other experts going to get the necessary experience in mid career when it is going to be AI that does much of the work?

Given the recent advances in AI evidenced by the performance of systems such as ChatGPT and GPT-4, it is likely that machines will be able to do almost all routine professional work. With the important caveat that they need to deliver a much greater degree of accuracy, processing of data with the new algorithms will give rise to alternative ways of delivering practical professional expertise.

As Susskind says, the professions risk becoming as outdated as the old liveries and crafts such as fletchers (arrow makers) and coopers (barrel makers).

In the UK, prompted by the 2017 Hall Pesenti Review[191] *Growing the artificial intelligence industry in the UK* and subsequently by the AI Council, much has happened in terms of the fostering of AI specialist skills. Turing Fellowships, AI-related PhDs, and conversion courses have been effectively funded and rolled out.

Our ability to attract and retain the top AI research talent, however, is also of paramount importance. Post Brexit, the cost of research visas is far higher than those in our Western counterparts and creates a real barrier to the future of UK research.

But the issues relating to digital skills and digital literacy go much wider than the high-end skills. As the AI Roadmap produced by the UK's AI Council in 2021[192] pointed out, the government needs to take steps to ensure that the general digital skills and digital literacy of the UK are brought up to speed.

A recent survey of small and medium-sized enterprises (SMEs), commissioned by the Open University for its report, *Skills for Success*, found that, while over 77% of SME leaders said their businesses do not have the required skills to successfully implement new technology, only 50% said that they have a plan to address these digital skills gaps within the next 12 months, with key barriers to intervention listed as time and cost.[193]

There is also the crucial importance of diversity in the technology workforce and research community. We must not build in the biases and prejudices of the past in the datasets we use, the algorithms we use, and the output of our AI systems. As a result, it is important that we have the necessary diversity/inclusion in the AI workforce which can help spot problems of bias in training data and decision-making.

The irony in terms of gender balance in the tech space, however, is that we have been going backwards since the Second World War and have only recently started to address the issue. The Lords AI Select Committee shared the priority expressed by the AI Council Roadmap for the achievement of greater diversity and inclusion in the AI workforce and wanted to see more progress. Little progress has been made in the intervening years, however, despite a number of initiatives from Women in AI, Women into Science and Engineering, the British Science Association, Tech Talent Charter, Tech London Advocates, and many others.[194]

The government itself needs to be taking much greater steps to encourage greater diversity in the training and recruitment of AI specialists.

So what skills should we be nurturing?

Futuredotnow,[195] founded by former Lord Mayor Sir Peter Estlin, in a roadmap published in July 2023 has estimated that 82% of today's jobs in the UK require digital skills but that 59% of the UK workforce is unable to do all of the digital tasks essential for work. They say that, on current estimates, essential digital skills gaps are costing the UK economy around £12.8 billion a year and the UK risks losing £145 billion in cumulative GDP growth up to 2028 due to inadequate digital skills.

It is very clear, however, this is not just that we should be developing STEM skills such as maths and coding. Tech developers agree that social and creative skills and critical thinking will be needed as well – human skills. So the humanities will be as important as the sciences in our schools. We need to teach the core skills required for children to flourish in the modern world, including critical thinking, verbal reasoning, and creativity.

The Royal Society, in their *Machine Learning* report, made a strong case for cross-disciplinary skills. Other skills include cross-cultural competency, novel and adaptive thinking and social intelligence. We need new active programmes to develop the skills that young people need. They also need much better information at the start of their working lives about the growth prospects for different sectors to be able to make career choices.

We are going to need creative skills, data-use skills, and innovation skills, but we may well not need quite so much in the way of analytical skills in the future, because that will be done for us.

As Dinah Caine, the Chair, said in her introduction to Camden's STEAM Commission report of 2017:

Going forward the development of Emotional Intelligence will be as critical as the development of Artificial Intelligence. And that is why the Commission recognises creativity as key to the fluid mix of skills that companies and individuals need to succeed in a rapidly changing environment.[196]

The jobs of the future have been aptly described by the former President and CEO of IBM, Ginni Rometty, as not about white collar vs. blue collar jobs, but about the 'new collar' jobs that employers in many industries demand, but which remain largely unfilled.

We are hiring because the nature of work is evolving – and that is also why so many of these jobs remain hard to fill. As industries from manufacturing to agriculture are reshaped by data science and cloud computing, jobs are being created that demand new skills – which in turn requires new approaches to education, training and recruiting….

And the surprising thing is that not all these positions require advanced education … What matters most is that these employees – with jobs such as cloud computing technicians and services delivery specialists – have relevant skills, often obtained through vocational training.[197]

The top skills currently being sought by business leaders as the latest Future Skills Report from the University of Kingston[198] has shown have a strong emphasis on critical thinking and creative skills as well as digital and analytical skills:

- Problem-solving – 69%
- Communication skills – 66%
- Digital skills – 61%
- Critical thinking – 60%
- Analytical skills – 57%
- Adaptability – 56%
- Initiative – 54%
- Relationship building – 53%
- Resilience – 53%
- Creativity – 52%

We also need to ensure that people have the opportunity to reskill and retrain to be able to adapt to the disruption in the labour market caused by AI. On that basis the author welcomes the recent introduction in the UK of a Lifelong Learning Entitlement[199] – designed to create a single funding system to help people train, retrain, and upskill flexibly over their working lives – and wants to see this built upon.

Particularly in the age of AI and automation, young people in particular need to be able to make informed choices about the type of jobs which will be available. We need to make sure that they don't simply have to learn where the opportunities are by trial and error. In the UK, careers advice and adult education need a total revamp. Apprentice levy reform is overdue. The work of Local Digital Skills Partnerships is welcome but they are massively under-resourced.

A significant government investment in skills and training particularly at further education level is imperative if disruption is to be navigated successfully and to the benefit of the working population and national productivity growth. Retraining will become a lifelong necessity. The UK government's Skills for Life Campaign[200] includes so-called skills bootcamps, targeted at adults aged over 19 looking to update or build their skills, including digital skills. Its Essential Digital Skills Framework measures and categorizes the basic digital skills needed. These are welcome, but with much chopping and changing in funding and organisation, including in the nature of qualifications gained, it is far from clear that there has been adequate and consistent focus in recent years on retraining and upskilling opportunities in the UK to meet the age of AI, or that these opportunities are adequately signposted.

The All-Party Parliamentary Group on Digital Skills, in their report mentioned earlier, in their conclusions included a number of aspects directly related to the availability of information on skills. They emphasised the need for an extensive database of materials and courses which could be used by both individuals and organisations to upskill and train themselves and their staff and for the provision available to be streamlined so individuals and organisations can clearly spot areas for development and access the opportunities available to them.[201] This is especially important given some of the very successful charity- and industry-led programmes available to boost digital skills which need signposting.[202]

Digital literacy

We need, however, to think beyond digital skills training and education, important though they are for employment and the economy. We need to take action on digital understanding. We must ensure that we know who has power over us and what values are in play when that power is exercised.

Broader digital literacy is crucial if we are to ensure that we are in the driving seat where AI is concerned. We need to learn how to live and work alongside AI and a specific training scheme should be designed to support people to work alongside AI and automation, and to be able to maximise their potential. This fits strongly with the recommendation of the AI Council's Roadmap back in 2021 for an online academy for understanding AI; they set a goal for every child leaving school to have a basic sense of how AI works.

At earlier stages of education in particular, children need to be adequately prepared for working with, and using, AI. For all children, the basic knowledge and understanding necessary to navigate an AI-driven world will be essential.

There is much good that technology can do but we must ensure that we know who has power over our children, and what values are in play when that power is exercised. This is vital for the future of our children, the proper functioning of our society, and the maintenance of public trust. We need to take action through personal, social, health, and economic (PSHE) education in schools as recommended by the *#StatusofMind* report from the Royal Society for Public Health (RSPH) report in 2017.[203]

Digital education is crucial. Schools need to teach children about these dangers, and how to use social media safely and responsibly. And parents must be empowered to protect their children online – including through digital literacy education, and advice and support for parents, too.

It is also crucial that adults, as well as children and young people, have better digital understanding. Anyone who has read Cathy O'Neil's book *Weapons of Math Destruction*, mentioned earlier, will be only too aware of the impact of algorithms on our lives already and the implications in particular for vulnerable and disadvantaged individuals and communities.

Some years ago, Doteveryone – the charity dedicated to responsible technology, sadly now no longer in operation – described what they called digital blindspots.[204] These were ignorance about:

- how adverts target us
- how our personal information is collected
- how prices can vary
- where our news comes from
- how products and services are paid for.

The UK had a vast literacy skills and knowledge gap, leaving the population at risk of harm. Full Fact's research in 2021[205] showed that one in three UK adults find it difficult to distinguish true information from false information. More widely, Ofcom found that 40% of UK adult internet users do not have the skills to critically assess online content. Just 2% of children in the UK have the critical thinking skills needed to tell fact from fiction online.[206]

There is also an unmet demand from citizens: Ipsos MORI and Google research in the same year[207] found that 55% of UK users want to learn more about how to use tools to distinguish between true and false information online, and two-thirds of users believed that internet and technology companies should provide training to improve the critical thinking of their users.

Good media and digital literacy is the first line of defence for us all from bad information online. It can make the difference between decisions based on sound evidence, and decisions based on poorly informed opinions that can harm health and well-being, social cohesion, and democracy. It is clear that there are a number of crucial components.

First, there is the need to understand the power of Big Data and what is known as Data Capitalism. Shoshana Zuboff in the title of her book, referred to earlier, gave it the name '*Surveillance Capitalism*'. What is being collected and when and what is it being used for, and who or what is it shared with? How long is it retained and when can it be expunged? Even so-called digital natives will not have an easy answer readily available.

We need to be able to look beneath the outer layer of the major internet companies to see what the consequences are of signing up to their standard terms. What redress do we have for misuse or breach of cybersecurity? Or for identity theft? What data are they collecting and sharing?

Second, we have the need for an understanding of the impact, sometimes beneficial, but also sometimes in a prejudicial way, of AI, machine learning, and of the algorithms that are employed on the data that is collected from us. Chatbots too, albeit currently less sophisticated than large language models, have been a growing feature of our lives – semi-autonomous interactive computer programs that mimic conversation with people using artificial intelligence.

Third, we need to understand how the digital world impacts our lives, how it affects the choices we make as citizens and the decisions that are made about and for us by business and government bodies, particularly in ways that affect us financially.

It is vital that, throughout, we treat AI as a tool and not as a technology that controls us. The greatest priority of all is the need to ensure public understanding. Public awareness of AI and machine learning is very low, even if what it delivers is recognised. It is clear that when there is awareness, there are a number of concerns expressed such as the fear they could cause harm, replace people, and skew the choices available. Public engagement – allied to regulation, as discussed later – is crucial to build trust in AI and machine learning.

During its existence Doteveryone strongly advocated public engagement to support digital understanding at all levels of society and with a specific focus on digital leadership for public institutions. That still remains a vital task.

In the UK, until the passing of the recent Online Safety Act,[208] Ofcom's obligations regarding media literacy and digital citizenship had remained unchanged since 2003, despite the massive changes that had taken place in technology since then. Amendments secured during the passage of the Act by campaigners and parliamentarians have updated Ofcom's media literacy duty under the UK's Communications Act 2003[209] to introduce new objectives relating specifically to social media and search platforms. In particular, Ofcom will be required to focus specifically on helping the public establish the reliability, accuracy, and authenticity of information they encounter online, and to understand how to better protect themselves and others from misinformation and disinformation.

Additionally, Ofcom will have to:

- publish a media literacy strategy every three years, and then report annually on their progress,
- publish recommendations for stakeholders, including tech companies and other organisations delivering media literacy initiatives, and
- undertake research to support their work.

In addition to this, however, a step change is needed in the focus and resources dedicated to media literacy in schools, supported by a plan for achieving clear measurable outcomes, and accountability for delivering it. The House of Lords Select Committee in 2021 in its report *Free for All? Freedom of Expression in the Digital Age*[210] recommended that digital citizenship should be a central part of the government's media literacy strategy, with proper funding. Digital citizenship education in schools should cover both digital literacy and conduct online, aimed at promoting civility and inclusion, and how it can be practised online. This should feature across subjects such as computing, PSHE and citizenship education.

In its response[211] the government cited its Media Literacy Framework of best practice principles,[212] which sets out the key skills and knowledge that are necessary for strong media literacy capabilities, and that the government believed should underpin media literacy initiatives with each of these principles seen as a core component of effective digital citizenship. They asserted that they were committed to increasing the amount of media literacy activity taking place in schools and that media literacy skills and knowledge are included throughout the national curriculum in numerous places.

Despite this, the All-Party Parliamentary Group on Media Literacy found in 2022[213] that 90% of the teachers surveyed wanted the national curriculum to specifically include media literacy, and it advocated updating the national curriculum and a Media Literacy Education Bill to drive the implementation of media literacy, with a designated Media Literacy Lead in educational establishments to ensure that a dedicated member of teaching staff oversees the implementation of a high-quality media literacy education, and the delivery of extracurricular media literacy activities.

Digital exclusion and data poverty

Then we have data poverty and digital exclusion. The shift to a digital economy has irreversibly changed the social and economic fabric of many societies. From a business perspective, the online world means lower barriers to entry, reduced costs, and increased access to markets both domestically and abroad through being able to operate online. The expansion of digital platforms has led to the emergence of new industries and job opportunities across AI, software, data analytics, social media, cybersecurity, biotechnology, robotics, financial technology, health tech, educational tech, and more. But there are clearly a great number of our citizens who cannot yet take advantage of these digital benefits. The identification of lack of access to devices and broadband and mobile connectivity is a major cause of data poverty.

Access to data affects every aspect of our lives – our ability to learn and to work, to connect with online public services, to access necessary services from banking to healthcare, and to socialise and connect with the people we know and love. For those with digital access, in terms of services in particular, this has been overwhelmingly positive, as access to the full benefits of state and society have never been more flexible or convenient. But this proved to be a major issue during the COVID pandemic – especially access to hardware, and mobile and broadband connectivity and digital skills – and the digital divide hasn't gone away subsequently.

Teach First, in particular, demonstrated the extent of digital exclusion among UK school children during the pandemic – 6% of parents had a child with no access to a device at all for home schoolwork – but the issues have not disappeared post pandemic.[214]

In the UK, the All-Party Parliamentary Group on Data Poverty (now renamed the Digital Inclusion APPG) and the House of Lords Communications and Digital Select Committee have recently highlighted the issues. In their report *Digital Exclusion* in 2023,[215] the Select Committee notes that 1.7 million households had no broadband or mobile internet access in 2021, and 2.4 million adults were unable to complete a simple basic task to get online, and 5 million workers will be acutely under-skilled in basic skills by 2030.

The Lloyds Bank UK Consumer Digital Index 2023[216] showed that the cost of digital access – as well as a lack of skills and will – means that 1 in 5 adults do not have the basic foundation-level digital skills to take full advantage of the digital world, and an Ofcom Adults' Media Use and Attitudes report of 2022[217] showed that 1 in 20 households do not have home internet access. Without further intervention, 5.8 million people are estimated to remain digitally excluded by the end of 2032.

Centre for Economics and Business Research (CEBR) research cited by the Good Things Foundation[218] estimates that for every £1 invested in interventions to enable digitally excluded people to build their basic digital skills, a return of £9.48 is gained throughout the economy, meaning that the UK economy is missing out on a net present value of £12.2 billion. The Local

Government Association's report on *The role of councils in tackling digital exclusion*[219] showed a strong relationship between having fixed broadband, and higher earnings and educational achievement, such as being able to work from home or for schoolwork. Each 10 percentage points increase in access to fixed broadband is associated with a 4 percentage point increase in the economic activity rate and about 3 points in the average Attainment 8 score at Key Stage 4.

So what are the key policies we should adopt?

As a start, we need an immediate improvement in government strategy and coordination. The government should play a key role in building inclusive digital economies but it is clear that there is little strategic guidance to councils from central government around tackling digital exclusion. As the Select Committee highlighted, the UK government's Digital Inclusion Strategy dates from 2014.[220] It is outdated and therefore is not something that councils refer to in shaping their local approaches to digital inclusion. So we need a new framework with national-level guidance, resources, and tools that support local digital inclusion initiatives.

The current strategy is bedevilled by the fact that responsibility spans several different government departments, so it is currently not clear who, if anyone, at ministerial and senior officer level has responsibility for coordinating the UK government's approach. The Select Committee was fairly scathing about new Department for Science, Innovation and Technology's claims to be treating digital inclusion as a priority in cross-Whitehall policymaking.

Therefore, there needs to be greater clarity around leadership as well as more explicit and effective mechanisms for coordinating government departments' efforts, to reduce duplication, for example on initiatives designed to improve access to devices and/or connectivity and help with digital skills.

Also, we should take on board many of Digital Inclusion APPG's recommendations for tackling data poverty in its *State of the Nation* Report of 2023, mentioned above, many of which are reinforced by the Select Committee's Report:

An agreed definition of data poverty – Government should convene stakeholders to agree a working definition of data poverty, and the Office for National Statistics should be mandated to start collecting relevant data for publication.

An assumed right to data – The Department for Science and Technology should put in place a legal assumption of the right to access data. This would drive support mechanisms from relevant departments, encourage internet service providers to do more, and stimulate the rollout of community-owned access points across the country (for example, in libraries or community centres).

A digital 'right-of-way' to public services – The government should put in place a statutory duty on all public bodies (such as NHS providers and schools) to ensure a digital 'right-of-way' solution so that users experiencing data poverty can still access digital-only services. For example, some GP surgeries will have iPads installed in their surgeries to provide a digital access point for their patients.

We all welcomed the introduction of social tariffs for broadband but the question of take-up needs addressing: we need to drive take-up. It is currently desperately low at 5%. One of the ways to do this is by social tariffs and data voucher auto-enrolment – the Department for Work and Pensions should work with internet service providers to create an auto-enrolment scheme for eligible households that includes one or both products as part of its Universal Credit package. The Select Committee also recommended that Ofcom should be empowered to regulate how and where companies advertise their social tariff.

Social tariff order journeys – In addition internet service providers should also have specific order journeys for customers seeking to sign up to a social tariff, with call centre staff given appropriate training to correctly authenticate the customers' universal credit status.

Making early termination free and simple – Internet service providers should waive early termination charges for customers moving onto universal credit and for customers already on universal credit but who could benefit from moving onto a social tariff with their current provider. Where ISPs already provide this service, they should make the necessary processes as simple and transparent as possible, and allow for switching to another provider's social tariff.

Creating a social inclusion fund – In the UK, VAT on broadband is charged at 20%, whereas for other goods and services deemed 'essential', it is charged at 5%. Broadband products should be deemed 'essential', with the 15% 'extra' charged on all broadband products (£2.1bn a year) ringfenced to make broadband affordable for all universal credit and pension credit (guaranteed credit) claimants. Community organisations could apply to access the databank, enabling them to provide data to people in their communities who need it.

There is also a strong role for local authorities in terms of local initiatives. As part of a properly resourced national strategy, city and county councils have a key role in driving an inclusive digital economy through:

- **Digitisation strategies**: Embedding digital inclusion throughout the council's other strategies, as a means of helping to deliver their intended outcomes.
- **Collaboration and partnerships**: Establishing mechanisms for cross-directorate information sharing and coordination in digital inclusion initiatives with other councils, and with tech companies.
- **Local economic support**: Ensuring that national-level resources are effectively leveraged for local benefit. These resources could be used to support local businesses and start-ups in the tech sector.
- **Digital skills development and training**: Offering digital skills courses and embedding digital skills in the school's curriculum.

At present, however, national support for digital exclusion is piecemeal. Local digital champions have a role to play in ensuring pockets of support can be picked up and utilised effectively, as well as pushing national bodies for more coordinated support packages. Two examples in major UK cities stand out in this respect.

100% Digital Leeds[221] is led by the digital inclusion team in the Integrated Digital Service (IDS) at Leeds City Council and Leeds Health and Care Partnership NHS West Yorkshire Integrated Care Board. It was launched as a blueprint for digital inclusion in the city backed by £2bn of funding, and tailored to the city's needs. The blueprint is based on the idea that local third-sector organisations are not always confident to deliver digital – or digital-inclusion – interventions, but are the ones who are closest to the communities that most need support. Dedicated digital champions help to build the confidence and capacity of these organisations to embed digital inclusion within their existing services. That includes helping them to find and apply for funding to deliver those interventions, funding that could be spent on additional staff, equipment, or connectivity.

Greater Manchester Combined Authority / Stockport Homes:[222] As of summer 2022, one in four Stockport Homes tenants were not online. Stockport carried out a large-scale survey to really get to grips with the digital challenges facing these tenants and found:

- Tenants who do not use the internet are more likely to be over 55 years of age, and have a disability or health condition, and/or have a pension as their main income.
- Even among those who are online, older residents and those with poor health have much more limited use and poorer skills than other households.
- Two-thirds rely on a mobile phone as their only device, fewer than 50% have a laptop, and 30% of households had no devices at all.

It was discovered that, of the residents who were online, two-thirds needed more information on social tariffs for broadband. A rolling month on month contract was the most popular option for data connectivity and 90% of respondents would need the tariff to be less than £15/month (most social tariffs are £15 or more at the moment).

However, in the author's view, we need to be even more ambitious and comprehensive in what we are trying to achieve in eliminating data poverty and digital exclusion. We need to think in terms of entitlement to a broader digital citizenship. As well as dealing with issues relating to data and freedom of speech, if adopted it should also encompass rights of access to connectivity and digital skills.

New employment rights

Furthermore, given the current and imminently greater disruption in the jobs market, we need to modernise employment rights to make them fit for the age of the AI-driven gig economy, to ensure that our employment laws protect the increasing number of workers whose lives can be ruled by algorithm without redress. The report *Gig Rights & Gig Wrongs: Initial Findings from the Gig Rights Project*[223] sets out clearly the job insecurity experienced by many of those in the digital economy. As they say, 'It is the centrality of digital platforms to the gig economy that renders it distinct from traditional forms of freelance, contract, and project-based work.' These include local platforms such as Deliveroo, Uber, TaskRabbit, Amazon Flex, and remote services such as Upwork and Fiverr.

Improving working conditions and security in our view means, in particular, establishing a new 'dependent contractor' employment status in between employment and self-employment, with entitlements to basic rights such as minimum earnings levels, sick pay, and holiday entitlement. It also means reviewing the tax and National Insurance status of employees, dependent contractors, and freelancers to ensure fair and comparable treatment.

More fundamentally we also believe that the use of AI systems for performance management in the workplace should be regulated. The campaigning organisation Foxglove has undertaken extensive research into Amazon's work practices in the UK in particular,[224] and found the extreme use of tracking software and the setting of stringent targets, in other words management by algorithm.

The Institute for the Future of Work, in a report with the All-Party Parliamentary Group on the Future of Work (APPGFOW), *The New Frontier: Artificial Intelligence at Work*, in November 2021[225] likewise pointed to significant negative impacts on the conditions and quality of work across the country from AI. Pervasive monitoring and target-setting technologies, in particular, are associated with pronounced negative impacts on mental and physical well-being as workers experience the extreme pressure of constant, real-time micro-management and automated assessment.

They recommended specific regulation for AI in the workplace centred around a proposal for an Accountability for Algorithms Act (AAA), an overarching, principles-driven framework for governing and regulating AI in response to the fast-changing developments in workplace technology. The AAA would include new rights and responsibilities, subject to a risk-based threshold, to ensure that all significant impacts from algorithmic decision-making on work or workers are considered and that appropriate action is always taken. This must be the right direction of travel.

7 The Case for Ethics-Oriented Governance and Regulation

Setting out the principles for AI development and adoption

The journey towards understanding the ethical underpinning needed for AI development and adoption has taken time. Concerned about lack of awareness of parliamentarians about the onset of AI and its implications for society, in late 2016, the author co-founded with Stephen Metcalfe MP, the All-Party Parliamentary Group on Artificial Intelligence, which is dedicated to informing parliamentarians about developments and to creating a community of interest around future policy regarding AI, its adoption, use, and regulation. He was then asked to chair the House of Lords Special inquiry Select Committee on AI with the remit 'to consider the economic, ethical and social implications of advances in artificial intelligence'.

As mentioned earlier, this produced its report *AI in the UK: Ready, Willing and Able?* in April 2018. It took a close look at government policy towards AI and its ambitions including those contained in the Hall Pesenti Review of October 2017 and those set out by former Prime Minister Teresa May in her Davos World Economic Forum Speech[226] including her goal for 'the UK to lead the world in deciding how AI can be deployed in a safe and ethical manner'.

The Committee did not, at that point, recommend any new regulatory body or AI-specific regulation but said that a framework of principles could underpin regulation, should it prove to be necessary in the future, and that existing regulators would be best placed to regulate AI in their respective sectors.

It took an optimistic view of the UK's potential, but also said that for successful development we needed to mitigate the risks such as the loss of public or stakeholder trust if AI was not seen to operate on ethical principles such as intelligibility, openness, fairness, and lack of bias.

The government in its response accepted the need to retain and develop public trust through an ethical approach both nationally and internationally.

The Hall Pesenti Review, mentioned earlier, was commissioned by the government, and it reported in late 2017. It had been tasked with reporting on the potential impact of AI on the UK economy, did not tackle the question of ethics or regulation of AI, but made a number of key recommendations designed to set a clear course for UK AI strategy.

The UK government's subsequent *Industrial Strategy: building a Britain fit for the future* published in November 2017,[227] identified putting AI 'at the forefront of the UK's AI and data revolution' as one of four 'Grand Challenges' identified as key to Britain's future and at the same time recognised that ethics would be key to the successful adoption of AI in the UK.

The *Industrial Strategy* led, in early 2018, to the establishment of a new Government Office for AI, designed to coordinate the implementation of the Hall Pesenti recommendations.

The Strategy and the Review also led to the establishment of the Centre for Data Ethics and Innovation (CDEI) in late 2018 with the remit 'to make sure that data and AI deliver the best possible outcomes for society, in support of their ethical and innovative use.'[228]

One of the main areas of focus of the Select Committee was the need to develop an appropriate ethical framework for the development and application of AI and it was an early advocate for international agreement on the principles to be adopted. The Select Committee concluded that the UK was in a strong position to be among the world leaders in the development of AI but it emphasised that if it was poorly handled, public confidence in AI could be undermined. It emphasised that the UK had a unique opportunity to forge a distinctive role for itself as a pioneer in ethical AI.

The Committee proposed five principles that could form the basis of a cross-sector AI code and which could be adopted nationally, and internationally.

- Artificial intelligence should be developed for the common good and benefit of humanity.

- Artificial intelligence should operate on principles of intelligibility and fairness.
- Artificial intelligence should not be used to diminish the data rights or privacy of individuals, families, or communities.
- All citizens should have the right to be educated to enable them to flourish mentally, emotionally, and economically alongside artificial intelligence.
- The autonomous power to hurt, destroy, or deceive human beings should never be vested in artificial intelligence.

In December 2020, the follow-up report *AI in the UK: No Room for Complacency*, referred to earlier, examined the progress made by the UK government. After interviews with government ministers, regulators, and other key players, our updated report made a number of key recommendations, in particular that the time had come for the UK government to move from deciding what the ethics were, to how to instil them in the development and deployment of AI systems. It called for the CDEI to establish and publish national standards for the ethical development and deployment of AI.

The Committee also concluded, relevant to AI governance and regulation, that:

- Greater public understanding was essential for the wider adoption of AI and active steps should be taken by government to explain to the general public the use of their personal data by AI.
- The development of policy to safeguard the use of data, such as Data Trusts, needed to pick up pace, otherwise it risked being left behind by technological developments.
- Users and policymakers needed to develop a better understanding of risk and how it can be assessed and mitigated, in terms of the context in which it is applied.

The Select Committee was not the first or the only one to advocate an ethical framework for the development of AI. In the runup, and subsequent to, the Lord's report there were numerous attempts to codify the key principles.

Principles	No of Principles	Year
Asimov's Law of Robotics	3	1950
Murphy and Wood's Three Laws of Responsible Robotics	3	2009
The EPSRC Principles of Robotics	5	2011
Tenets: Partnership on AI	8	2016
Future of Life Institute's Asilomar Principles for Beneficial AI	23	Jan 2017
ACM US Public Policy Council's Principles for Algorithmic Transparency and Accountability	7	Jan 2017
Japanese Society for Artificial Intelligence (JSAI) Ethical Guidelines	9	Feb 2017
Draft principles of the Future Society's Science Law and Society Initiative	6	Oct 2017
Montreal Declaration for Responsible AI	7	Nov 2017
IEEE General Principles of Ethical Autonomous and Intelligent Systems	5	Dec 2017
UNI Global Union Top 10 Principles for Ethical AI	5	Dec 2017
House of Lords Select Committee	5	April 2018
Ethics Guidelines for Trustworthy AI: EU High Level Expert Group on Artificial Intelligence	9	April 2019
Beijing Principles	15	May 2019
OECD Recommendations of the Council on Artificial Intelligence	5	May 2019
G20	5	June 2019

Without a doubt the most influential have been the five core principles set out in the OECD guidelines for responsible stewardship of trustworthy AI, designed to promote artificial intelligence (AI) adopted in May 2019.[229]

These are:

1. Inclusive growth, sustainable development, and well-being

Stakeholders should proactively engage in responsible stewardship of trustworthy AI in pursuit of beneficial outcomes for people and the planet, such as augmenting human capabilities and enhancing creativity, advancing inclusion of underrepresented populations, reducing economic, social, gender and other inequalities, and protecting natural environments, thus invigorating inclusive growth, sustainable development and well-being.

2. Human-centred values and fairness

AI actors should respect the rule of law, human rights and democratic values, throughout the AI system lifecycle. These include freedom, dignity and autonomy, privacy and data protection, non-discrimination and equality, diversity, fairness, social justice, and internationally recognised labour rights. To this end, AI actors should implement mechanisms and safeguards, such as capacity for human determination, that are appropriate to the context and consistent with the state of art.

3. Transparency and explainability

AI actors should commit to transparency and responsible disclosure regarding AI systems. To this end, they should provide meaningful information, appropriate to the context, and consistent with the state of art:

  i.   *to foster a general understanding of AI systems,*
  ii. *to make stakeholders aware of their interactions with AI systems, including in the workplace,*
  iii. *to enable those affected by an AI system to understand the outcome, and,*

    iv.   *to enable those adversely affected by an AI system to challenge its outcome based on plain and easy-to-understand information on the factors, and the logic that served as the basis for the prediction, recommendation or decision.*

4. Robustness, security and safety

    a)   *AI systems should be robust, secure and safe throughout their entire lifecycle so that, in conditions of normal use, foreseeable use or misuse, or other adverse conditions, they function appropriately and do not pose unreasonable safety risk.*

    b)   *To this end, AI actors should ensure traceability, including in relation to datasets, processes and decisions made during the AI system lifecycle, to enable analysis of the AI system's outcomes and responses to inquiry, appropriate to the context and consistent with the state of art.*

    c)   *AI actors should, based on their roles, the context, and their ability to act, apply a systematic risk management approach to each phase of the AI system lifecycle on a continuous basis to address risks related to AI systems, including privacy, digital security, safety and bias.*

5. Accountability

AI actors should be accountable for the proper functioning of AI systems and for the respect of the above principles, based on their roles, the context, and consistent with the state of art.

This then led the following month to the adoption by the G20 at its meeting in Osaka of non-binding principles for responsible stewardship of trustworthy AI which reflected those of the OECD.[230]

In 2021 all 193 Member States of UNESCO adopted a global standard on AI ethics, the *Recommendation on the Ethics of Artificial Intelligence*.[231] These included:

    • *Proportionality and do no harm – AI systems must be appropriate to the context*

- *Safety and security*
- *Fairness and non-discrimination*
- *Sustainability*
- *Right to privacy and data protection*
- *Human oversight and determination*
- *Transparency and explainability*
- *Responsibility and accountability*
- *Awareness and literacy*
- *Multistakeholder and adaptive governance and collaboration – governance needs to be internationally interoperable.*

After the G7 summit in Hiroshima, in October 2023 agreement on International Guiding Principles for Organizations Developing Advanced AI Systems and an International Code of Conduct for Organizations Developing Advanced AI Systems was reached.[232] The voluntary guidance, building on a 'Hiroshima AI Process', aims to promote safe, secure, trustworthy AI. The principles are more prescriptive and practical than previous sets of ethical guidelines, based as they are on the recent development of powerful generative AI systems.[233]

Organisations developing the most advanced AI systems are urged to abide by the following principles, 'commensurate to the risks':

1 Take appropriate measures throughout the development of advanced AI systems, including prior to and throughout their deployment and placement on the market, to identify, evaluate, mitigate risks across the AI lifecycle.

2 Identify and mitigate vulnerabilities, and, where appropriate, incidents and patterns of misuse, after deployment including placement on the market.

3 Publicly report advanced AI systems' capabilities, limitations, and domains of appropriate and inappropriate use, to support ensuring sufficient transparency.

4 Work towards responsible information sharing and reporting of incidents among organizations developing advanced AI systems including with industry, governments, civil society, and academia.

5 Develop, implement and disclose AI governance and risk management policies, grounded in a risk-based approach – including privacy policies, and mitigation measures, in particular for organizations developing advanced AI systems.

6 Invest in and implement robust security controls, including physical security, cybersecurity and insider threat safeguards across the AI lifecycle. These may include securing model weights and algorithms, servers, operational security measures for information security and appropriate cyber/physical access controls.

7 Develop and deploy reliable content authentication and provenance mechanisms such as watermarking or other techniques to enable users to identify AI-generated content.

8 Prioritize research to mitigate societal, safety and security risks and prioritize investment in effective mitigation measures.

9 Prioritize the development of advanced AI systems to address the world's greatest challenges, notably but not limited to the climate crisis, global health and education.

10 Advance the development of and, where appropriate, adoption of international technical standards.

11 Implement appropriate data input controls and audits.

In the years subsequent to the agreement on the OECD principles, much work has been done at international level in the Council of Europe, OECD, EU, and a number of major jurisdictions such as China, the UK, and USA towards putting ethical principles into practice. Regulation has not necessarily been the only solution.

There are, in our view, three layers to the ethical governance of AI which are crucial to understanding where regulation fits in this process.

First, the setting out of ethical principles, such as those adopted by the OECD and UNESCO, to which AI systems should conform at a high level of generality.

Below that level of generality can come the legislative teeth, the framework which dictates the extent to which the principles must, by law, be enshrined in AI systems. In practice, this will be a question of how far standards set for tools such as risk and impact assessment, audit, training, testing, and monitoring are obligatory for developers and adopters, and the context and conditions under which these tools need to be deployed.

At the lowest level of generality – specifically intended to encapsulate the ethical AI principles – are the standards to be adopted. These can be variously applied to the tools used to test and audit AI, to ensure the safety of AI systems and assess their attendant risks and impact. Standards can be created domestically but unlike legislation and regulation they are much more adapted to international agreement. Above all, this means agreeing on standards for risk and impact assessments and testing alongside tools for audit and continuous monitoring for higher-risk applications.

The EU, the UK, and the US have each sought to approach the governance of technology in several distinct forms relative to these three layers, and this is explored in more detail in the next chapter.

Legal AI liability accountability and redress

It is clear that one of the grey areas of AI development and adoption is the question of legal liability. It follows that there need to be standards of accountability and redress which are readily understood.

In 2016, the CEO of Microsoft, Satya Nadella,[234] urged creators to take accountability for the algorithms they create, given the possible unintended consequences, which only they could solve. This raises a whole range of issues, and Chris Reed, Professor of Electronic Commerce Law at the Centre for Commercial Law Studies, Queen Mary University of London has outlined the essence of legal Accountability in terms of:

- Explainability and transparency
- Remediability
- Responsibility
- Verifiability.[235]

Without venturing into the world of autonomous vehicles, which raises the whole spectrum of legal accountability issues in itself, the concept of

Accountability and with it, Responsibility and Remediability in particular, mean that our complaints and disputes resolution systems must be fit for purpose. The traditional role of the ombudsman in helping to create fairer markets which work for consumers as well as businesses needs to be rethought. The provision of utilities is increasingly governed by algorithms, as will also be the case with the Internet of Things.

Systemic issues in markets such as telecommunications and energy are at risk of becoming exacerbated as big data and AI provide the conditions for the proliferation of opaque, scalable, and unfair approaches to consumer rights. If ombudsman schemes are to continue to be effective in improving business practice and in tackling consumer detriment, then their role and capabilities must change. These schemes must understand and engage with issues of fairness in an emerging digital world – taking a more systemic and preventative view and providing assurance around appropriate redress.

The EU itself in 2022 started on the road towards establishing the legal liability framework for AI systems through its proposal for a Liability Directive on the express basis that current national liability rules, in particular based on fault, are not suited to handling liability claims for damage caused by AI-enabled products and services and to ensure that 'victims of damage caused by AI obtain equivalent protection to victims of damage caused by products in general'.[236]

Complaint handling in this respect needs to transform over the next decade, and it is essential that the risks for vulnerable consumers are properly considered and that compassion and fairness are not compromised by new technology.

Corporate governance and AI

Even when specific regulation or legislation have not yet come into play it is clear that AI – even in its narrow form – will have a profound impact on, and implications for, corporate governance. Global organisations such as the Partnership on AI[237] recognise that corporate responsibility and governance on AI, in line with a set of principles, is increasingly important. Likewise, this is the view of the World Economic Forum (WEF), which has a long track record of involvement in AI governance and, over time, has developed a substantial amount of AI corporate governance guidance and tools.[238]

Detailed guidance is available too on a country-by-country basis. In 2019, Singapore launched its *Model AI Governance Framework*.[239] In the UK in the same year, the Institute for Business Ethics issued a masterly briefing for boards: *Corporate Ethics in a Digital Age*.[240] Investors in the US and the UK, such as Analytics Ventures, Fidelity, and Hermes, have also set out their own governance expectations.

Likewise, the Tech Faculty of the Institute of Chartered Accountants in England and Wales (ICAEW) produced a valuable paper on *New Technologies, Ethics and Accountability*.[241] They stressed that companies need to operationalise the ethics and engrain ethical behaviour.

Poor data governance is often at the heart of public mistrust, but there is a wide range of actions that boards need to take, beyond complying with data protection legislation such as the UK's General Data Protection Regulation (GDPR) and data protection and privacy legislation applicable in other jurisdictions.

Boards must have the right skill sets to understand what technology is being used in their company and how it is being used and managed, in order to fulfil their oversight role. Do board members understand whether and how AI is being used and managed, for instance by their HR department in recruitment and assessment or in keeping track of employee movements?

Understanding the different aspects of business context in which AI can impact is crucial. How many boards appreciate the full range of applications of AI which are available?

Boards need to ensure that they are informed about the implications of the automation of many tasks before deployment of AI solutions takes place. Will the introduction of an AI solution augment a role or substitute for it?

Companies need to be transparent about the impact of AI solutions on their workforces and on decision-making. They need to accept that they are fully accountable where the introduction of new technology has a significant impact on employees and customers.

Whatever the scale of introduction of AI, there will be major disruption in the workplace, and concerted retraining to meet the demand for new skills will become a major and continuing necessity.

Conformity with ethical principles and standards, of course, has to be central to the introduction of new technology. If boards are going to retain stakeholder trust they need to adopt an overarching ethics framework that ensures that certain principles on the deployment of AI solutions are followed, such as beneficial purpose, personal privacy, transparency of use, that data being used for training, testing, or operational inputting does not exhibit bias and that algorithmic decision-making is explainable.

However, as a WEF Insight report said in 2021[242] 'Principles are important, but the only way to adhere to them is by developing the sound practices, tools and systems that make it easy for the people who have to build and use them.'

In sum, even in advance of specific AI legislation and regulation, boards need to be aware of the questions that they should ask and the advice that they need, and from whom, when considering the adoption of AI solutions.

- Does the board have the right skills and knowledge to consider the risks and issues?
- Does it understand how data, algorithms, and other technologies are being used in the business, especially to make key decisions or predictions?
- How is ethics around technology included within board governance? How often is ethics and technology discussed by the board?
- Does the business include oversight of compliance with ethics in the remit of its Audit and Risk committee or set up a separate Ethics Advisory Board?
- How is the board communicating the importance of an ethical approach to AI adoption? How are new staff taught about the ethical values of the business?
- Has the board received assurance that any ethical risks around the adoption of new technology are being managed? Is ethics considered when reviewing or signing off new AI projects or use cases?
- Furthermore, if AI solutions are externally sourced, are these ethical requirements engrained in procurement processes?

- Are appropriate accountabilities in place? How does accountability between the business leadership and technology specialists fit together? Who is accountable at board level for these issues?
- What tools does the business have available in exercising oversight in terms of AI risk assessment and ethical audit mechanisms?.
- Has the board, in seeking assurance on the standards for training, testing, and operation of AI systems to be deployed, considered all relevant tools?
- What domestic and international standards for AI development are relevant to its use of AI systems?
- Risk management is central to the introduction of new technology such as AI. What is the risk appetite of the business for the adoption of new technologies? How is risk assessed?
- To what extent are 'unexplainable' models relied on in decision-making? Developers and those applying AI solutions should not shelter behind 'black box' excuses.
- Where there is automated decision-making, to what extent have controls been reviewed to ensure that there is a 'human in the loop'?
- To what extent should individual AI system designers and engineers within the business be explicitly required to declare their adherence to a set of ethical standards? This is particularly relevant to AI developers.
- Importantly, is the board satisfied that they have the necessary diversity and inclusion in the AI workforce, with different perspectives, when developing technology which enables them to spot problems of bias in training data and decision-making?
- Are there mechanisms for employees to raise concerns about ethical questions, such as whistleblowing processes?
- Is the business open and engaged with key stakeholders around ethics and technology? To what extent has the business published its ethical approach and engaged customers and others in discussions and feedback?
- Where the business is regulated, to what extent is it engaged in discussions with regulators about any changing requirements?

- Is there recognition of the potential role for regulatory sandboxing, as a number of regulators such as the UK's Financial Conduct Authority and the Information Commissioner's Office in particular have recognised and promoted? This permits the testing of a new technology without the threat of regulatory enforcement but with strict overview and guidance and can speed up innovation and scaling up of adoption of AI projects.[243]

The corporate challenge of generative AI

Generative AI has provided new governance challenges to organisations.

A number of developers of generative AI systems at the instigation of the White House have agreed to a set of voluntary AI commitments[244] or endorsed the G7's International Code of Conduct for Advanced AI Systems regarding their development and use, mentioned earlier, but this is not an issue for developers alone. The US film and television industry, as part of the settlement of the actors' and writers' strike mentioned earlier, will need to adhere to agreements about the use of AI systems impacting on their livelihoods.[245] Organisations such as the BBC[246] have reflected this in early public adoption of three guiding principles that undertake the BBC 'will always act in the public's best interests, prioritise talent and creativity by respecting the rights of artists, and be open and transparent about AI-made output'. The Associated Press too has issued guidelines on how to use it.[247]

More broadly, the need for internal corporate guidance stems from the potential risks arising from use of standard publicly available systems such as ChatGPT by employees. These include the risks described earlier such as hallucinations and overdependence, but also introduce new risks such as ingestion of confidential corporate information which could be accessed by competitors. This has led to the adoption of strong corporate codes of conduct on the use of these systems, and guidance on the drawing up of usage policies is now increasingly available.[248]

The opportunity for change

However, there are even broader issues to be addressed. The rise of AI marks a real opportunity for radical changes in corporate governance on a global basis. Many of the above questions raise the issue of what the core ethical values of the business are and how they fit with its current business model and strategy.

In our view, AI can and should contribute positively to a purposeful form of capitalism that is not simply the pursuit of profit but where companies deploy AI in an ethical way for the purpose of achieving greater sustainability. With all the potential opportunities and disruption involved with AI, boards across a variety of jurisdictions and business contexts need to adopt a strong underlying set of corporate values so that the impact and distribution of benefit to employees and society at large are fully considered for a purpose not exclusively driven by returns to shareholders.

In this context, Sir Ronald Cohen, Co-founder and Chair of the Global Steering Group for Impact Investment, at CogX2020[249] in London spoke about the need for a 'universal impact accounting system'. In the same year the WEF published Integrated Corporate Governance: *A Practical Guide to Stakeholder Capitalism for Boards of Directors*[250] which emphasised that:

> *the COVID-19 pandemic and resulting humanitarian and economic crisis have reminded us that firms are themselves stakeholders in the sense that they have an intrinsic interest in and shared responsibility for the resilience and vitality of the economic, social and environmental systems in which they operate.*

The Big Innovation Centre, under the Chairmanship of Will Hutton, has played a leading role in the debate with their 'Purposeful Company Project'[251] which was launched back in 2015 with an ethos that 'the role of business is to fulfil human wants and needs and to pursue a purpose that has a clear benefit to society. It is through the fulfilment of their chosen purpose that value is created.' Since then, they have produced several important reports on the need for an integrated regulatory approach to stewardship and intrinsic purpose definition.

The B Corp movement,[252] which is now global and has a presence in 92 countries, has been a leader in this strongly growing community of interest, determined to raise standards of corporate governance. Certified B Corporations, or B Corps, are companies verified by B Lab to meet high standards of social and environmental performance, transparency, and accountability.

Next steps

Corporate governance, however sound, is not always going to be sufficient. Many business leaders are absolutely aware of the need for good corporate behaviour but at the end of the day ethical principles and good corporate responsibility guidelines may not be enough. It has become clear that voluntary ethical guidelines, however much they are widely shared, are not enough to guarantee ethical AI. The question now is how to bridge the gap between corporate behaviour and regulatory intervention. That takes us on to discussing how far we need to go in adopting legislation and regulation specific to AI.

8 The Role of Regulation: Patchwork Quilt or Fishing Net?

Embedding ethical principles through regulation

It is clear that, as it stands in most jurisdictions, coverage in law which would ensure that AI systems reflect the OECD principles is very patchy. Bias may be covered by existing equality legislation, data issues by data protection laws, but there is no existing obligation for ethics by design ensuring transparency, explainability, and accountability. Liability for the performance of AI systems is also unclear.

If only partial, regulation risks becoming a patchwork quilt, guiding principles, and governmental guidance that will allow even risky AI applications to slip through the net. There will be regulatory grey areas where neither developer nor adopter know what laws and standards they need to apply and when. It is at this level where differing cultural approaches to regulation are most in evidence.[253]

The EU approach

The EU started on its route towards AI regulation with the adoption of a European AI Strategy[254] in 2018 and the appointment of a high-level expert group (HLEG) on artificial intelligence in 2019.[255] HLEG made recommendations on future-related policy developments including Ethics Guidelines for Trustworthy Artificial Intelligence with their 'human-centric approach' on AI.

Since then the EU has elected to take the strategy forward by adopting a comprehensive approach to AI regulation with a combination of binding regulations and guiding directives designed to ensure that AI systems are safe, and respect fundamental rights and EU values. The AI Act which at the time of writing is in the process of being adopted by the EU, is built on principles developed by HLEG, very similar to those adopted by the OECD, but then it sets out how these are to be achieved.

In essence, the Act is designed to regulate AI, based on AI's capacity to cause harm to society, following a 'risk-based' approach which means that the higher the risk, the stricter the rules that have to be followed. The EU is also thereby consciously attempting to set a global standard for AI regulation in other jurisdictions, just as the GDPR has done.

Adopters and developers of AI systems classified as high risk (for example, medical devices, power tools, use in the context of recruitment or employment, use in education, or use in credit scoring for lending) must carry out a fundamental rights impact assessment before a high-risk AI system is put in the market by its deployers. There will be quality rules for training, validation, and testing datasets, and a need to set in place additional transparency rules to ensure that these systems are legally compliant, ethically sound, and technically robust.

Providers of high-risk AI systems must maintain records of programming and training methodologies, datasets used, and measures taken for oversight and control.

AI systems presenting only limited risk, however, will be subject to a light transparency obligation, for example disclosing that the content was AI-generated so that users can make informed decisions on further use.

The main new elements included in the final negotiations on the Act[256] are:

- New rules on high-impact general-purpose AI models that can cause systemic risk in the future, as well as on high-risk AI systems.
- A revised system of governance with some enforcement powers at EU level.
- Better protection of rights through the obligation for deployers of high-risk AI systems to conduct a fundamental rights impact assessment prior to putting an AI system into use.

The list of prohibitions, i.e. the AI systems deemed to fall into the category of unacceptable risk, was also extended. In general, the following will be prohibited:

- Biometric categorisation systems that use sensitive characteristics (e.g. political, religious, philosophical beliefs, sexual orientation, race).
- Untargeted scraping of facial images from the internet or CCTV footage to create facial recognition databases.
- Emotion recognition in the workplace and educational institutions.
- Social scoring based on social behaviour or personal characteristics.
- AI systems that manipulate human behaviour to circumvent their free will.
- AI used to exploit the vulnerabilities of people (due to their age, disability, social, or economic situation).

These will, however, be subject to a national security exception. Also, biometric categorisation will be subject to certain exceptions, such as law enforcement, where this search is to identify a victim or suspect from an existing lawfully acquired database. AI profiling systems, however, cannot be used by the police for making assessments of the risk of a person committing a criminal offence. The same prohibition, subject to medical or safety exception, applies to AI systems used for emotion recognition. Real-time and post remote biometric identification by law enforcement authorities in publicly accessible spaces will be subject to prior authorisation by a judicial or independent administrative authority. Private use will be considered high risk.

Exclusively military or defence or national security purposes are excluded. So too are AI systems used for the sole purpose of research and innovation, or by people using AI for non-professional reasons.

There will also be established an EU database in which AI systems should be registered, including high-risk AI systems deployed by or on behalf of public authorities, except for high-risk AI systems used for law enforcement purposes or in the field of migration.

The definition of AI in the Act aligns with the new definition proposed by the OECD, which is cited in Chapter 2. The revised Act will also clarify the relationship between responsibilities under the AI Act and responsibilities that already exist under other legislation, such as the relevant EU data protection or sectoral legislation.

The Act will also address the specific case of high-impact general-purpose AI (GPAI) systems and foundation models – defined as models whose training required 1025 FLOPS (floating-point operations per second) of computing power – basically the largest of the large language models, which can be used for multiple purposes with an AI Office set up within the Commission to oversee them. Inter alia developers will be required to conduct model evaluations, assess and mitigate systemic risks, conduct adversarial testing, report to the Commission on serious incidents, ensure cybersecurity, and report on their energy efficiency.

Non-compliance with the Act will lead to substantial fines, ranging from €35 million or 7% of global turnover to €7.5 million or 1.5% of turnover, depending on the infringement and company size. Consumers and citizens will have the right to launch complaints and receive meaningful explanations about decisions based on high-risk AI systems that impact their rights.

If the final form of the Act is agreed during 2024, it will come into effect two years later, in 2026.

AI governance in the US

In the US, the main initiatives on AI governance and regulation have come from the White House, under successive administrations of Presidents Obama, Trump, and Biden, generally lacking the force of law passed by Congress, but with one measure, the National Artificial Intelligence Initiative Act of 2020, having as one of its key objectives 'To lead the world in the development and use of trustworthy AI systems in the public and private sectors' and setting up a National Artificial Intelligence Initiative Office and National Artificial Intelligence Advisory Committee.[257]

In 2022, the White House Office of Science Technology Policy (OSTP) released a document entitled *Blueprint for an AI Bill of Rights: Making Automated Systems Work for the American People*.[258] Specifically, senior White House leaders called upon policymakers to 'codify these measures into law or use the framework and its technical companion to help develop specific guidance on the use of automated systems within a sector.' In the Bill of Rights, officials provide 'a set of five principles and associated practices to help guide the design, use, and deployment of automated systems to protect the rights of the American public in the age of artificial intelligence.' The core protections to which everyone should be entitled include:

- Safe and effective systems.
- Algorithmic discrimination protections to ensure that systems are designed and used in an equitable way.
- Data privacy protections that are 'built-in' and allow people better control over how data about themselves is used.
- Notice and explanation, so that users are aware that automated systems are being used and understand their potential impact.
- The right to opt out of automated decision-making 'in favor of a human alternative, where appropriate' and to have 'access to timely human consideration and remedy by a fallback and escalation process if an automated system fails, it produces an error, or you would like to appeal or contest its impacts on you.'

The intention, set out in some detail, was for a wide range of federal agencies to consider and develop new rules and guidance governing various sectors of the US economy. Congress was encouraged to use the framework as a resource in codifying these into law.

The White House emphasised that the principles were not targeted only at public-sector policymakers. Project managers, workers, parents, and healthcare providers were among stakeholders to be encouraged to use the new framework in assessing AI systems and products and advocating to 'ensure that innovation is rooted in inclusion, integrity, and our common humanity'.

Following this and giving greater force to the Blueprint, in terms of practical and enforceable obligations, has been the Biden Administration's Executive Order on Safe, Secure, and Trustworthy Artificial Intelligence, issued in the autumn of 2023,[259] setting out comprehensive regulation of its use in the federal government. The new Executive Order requires many federal agencies to develop and deploy guidance, oversight frameworks, and other governance mechanisms aimed at monitoring and ensuring that the use and deployment of AI adheres to existing federal law. It is broadly aimed at advancing a coordinated federal-government-wide approach to the safe and responsible development and use of AI. The order at the outset first outlines several overarching principles and goals for the development and deployment of AI and then provides mandates to a number of primary administrative agencies regarding particular actions that must be taken to ensure that AI is developed and deployed responsibly, equitably, and in compliance with federal law.

The Order begins by describing eight principles that govern the federal government's development and use of AI while guiding the oversight of entities operating in the private sector. The eight principles are:

- Ensuring the Safety and Security of AI technology
- Promoting Innovation and Competition
- Supporting Workers
- Advancing Equity and Civil Rights
- Protecting Consumers, Patients, Passengers, and Students
- Protecting Privacy
- Advancing Federal Government Use of AI
- Strengthening American Leadership Abroad.

The Order then moves into a broad directive apportionment to a great many administrative agencies. It covers all types of AI, particularly 'dual-use foundation models'. As defined by the Order, a dual-use foundation model is an AI model which is:

trained on broad data, generally uses self-supervision, contains at least tens of billions of parameters, is applicable across a wide range of contexts, and that exhibits, or could be easily modified to exhibit, high levels of performance at tasks that pose a serious risk to security, national economic security, national public health or safety, or any combination of those matters.

A large part of the Executive Order is dedicated to dispensing mandates aimed at mitigating societal harms posed by the use and development of

AI, with particular focus on unintended bias and discrimination potentially produced by the use of AI and other algorithmic systems.

As yet no AI governance measure has made its way through Congress, although there have been a number of attempts to do so. The most recent is the Artificial Intelligence Research, Innovation, and Accountability Act of 2023 (AIRIA)[260] which has bipartisan support from members of the Senate Commerce Committee, which holds jurisdiction over agencies overseeing AI, such as the National Institute for Standards and Technology (NIST).

The AIRIA is broadly split into two themes. As well as encouraging innovation, it is designed to establish a framework of accountability, including reporting obligations, risk-management assessment protocols, certification procedures, enforcement measures, and a push for wider consumer education on AI. The core of the legislation rests on new transparency and certification requirements for AI system deployers based on two categories of AI systems: i) 'high-impact' and ii) 'critical-impact'. The legislation would establish a new certification regime for AI, requiring critical-impact artificial intelligence systems to self-certify compliance with standards developed by the Department of Commerce. The AIRIA would also require transparency reports to be provided to the Department of Commerce in sectors of housing, employment, credit, education, healthcare, and insurance.

It is clear that senior legislators from both parties are making AI governance a priority. AIRIA is perhaps the most comprehensive AI legislation introduced to date in the US Congress and represents a major step towards legislation governing AI in the US.

EU and US common ground?

With the publication of the White House's Executive Order (EO) we can start to see the areas of common ground and difference between the US approach to AI regulation and that set out in the most recent drafts of the EU's AI Act.

A key distinction between the EO and the current drafts of the AI Act lies in their reach. Not waiting for Congress to pass law to regulate private industry directly, the EO draws on the power of the Presidency to require federal executive departments across sectors to formulate industry standards, guidelines, practices, and regulations for AI development and usage. In contrast, the AI Act aims to establish a regulatory framework for artificial intelligence across the entire EU, as a single horizontal regulation with direct impact for the private sector. As an EU Regulation, it will be directly applicable in all EU Member States, without the need of local implementation, except for aspects specifically provided within the AI Act.

The EO predominantly focuses on standards and guidelines, while the AI Act enforces binding regulations, violations of which will incur fines and other penalties without further legislative action.

The AI Act takes a use-case-based approach to regulating AI. As described earlier the AI Act defines a small number of prohibited practices, and a longer list of 'high-risk' use cases. The AI Act will also set out controls on the deployment of 'foundation models', such as large language models or image generation AIs, which can be used in many different AI systems or workflows. Similarly, the EO pays special attention to so-called 'dual-use foundation models'.

Both the AI Act and the EO underscore system testing and monitoring across an AI system's lifecycle. The AI Act requires businesses to substantiate their compliance, incorporating comprehensive pre-market testing procedures and adopt a policy for post-market monitoring of the system's continued performance. Likewise, the EO contemplates that:

> *testing and evaluations, including post-deployment performance monitoring, will help ensure that AI systems function as intended, are resilient against misuse or dangerous modifications, are ethically developed and operated in a secure manner, and are compliant with applicable Federal laws and policies.*

However, although there is substantial overlap between the AI Act and the EO's requirements, the EU's approach is essentially based on a formal demonstration of compliance, while in the US alignment with industry standards might be enough to comply with it.

Understanding the common ground that underpins these two superficially disparate regimes is key to developing a future compliance strategy that allows global organisations to align with both. How this can be developed for future international compliance strategies is discussed later.

AI governance in the UK

The UK's journey was initially promising. A long gestation period of national AI policymaking which started so well back in 2017 with the Hall Pesenti Review has, however, ended up producing a minimalist approach to AI regulation.

A number of institutions such as the ICO, Alan Turing Institute, Centre for Data Ethics and Innovation, and the Office for AI – the latter two, as mentioned, were both the consequence of the Hall Pesenti Review – worked together to develop, roll out, and monitor training for regulators on issues around AI. The Office for AI was an active force in the field with its *Guidelines for AI Procurement*[261] and the government published a Framework for High-Stakes Algorithmic Decision-Making in the Public Sector, both mentioned earlier.

The Centre for Data Ethics and Innovation published numerous reports such as on bias in algorithmic decision-making which focused on a number of particular sectors and on online targeting, used to promote and personalise content and to target advertising, Snapshots on Deepfakes and AudioVisual Disinformation, AI and Personal Insurance and Smart Speakers and Voice Assistants and publication of its AI Barometer described as a 'major analysis of the most pressing opportunities, risks and governance challenges associated with AI and data use in the UK'.[262]

The Alan Turing Institute played a major role in collaboration across the AI landscape nationally and internationally, including bringing together 400 fellows, in the ExplAIn project with the ICO[263] and in developing policy with the OECD and Council of Europe. A number of UK regulators such as the Financial Conduct Authority and the Information Commissioner's Office led the way on regulatory sandboxing. Even GCHQ – the UK's intelligence, security and cyber agency – produced a set of AI ethics for their operations.[264]

Most importantly, the UK's National AI strategy – a ten-year plan for

UK investment in and support of AI – was then published in September 2021,[265] which accepted the fact that in the UK we needed:

- to prepare for artificial general intelligence
- to establish public trust and trustworthy AI
- the government to set an example in its use of AI
- international standards for AI development and use.

It also proposed an ecosystem of AI assurance tools, acknowledging that for regulators, developers, and adopters the development of AI technical standards (foundational, process, and measurement) – particularly international ones – is important for AI assurance. Although not a regulator, the CDEI then produced its *Roadmap to an effective AI assurance ecosystem*,[266] in December 2021, in which it emphasised the need for independently agreed standards for tools such as audit, conformity assessment, and certification to work effectively.

In a subsequent *AI Policy Paper and AI Action Plan*,[267] published in July 2022, the UK government set out its emerging proposals for regulating AI, in which it committed to develop 'a pro-innovation national position on governing and regulating AI' to be set out in a subsequent AI Governance White Paper.

Their approach was to be:

Establishing clear, innovation-friendly and flexible approaches to regulating AI will be core to achieving our ambition to unleash growth and innovation while safeguarding our fundamental values and keeping people safe and secure. … drive business confidence, promote investment, boost public trust and ultimately drive productivity across the economy.

To facilitate its 'pro-innovation' approach, the government proposed several early cross-sectoral and overarching principles that built on the OECD Principles on Artificial Intelligence, and were to be interpreted and implemented by regulators within the context of the environment they oversee and therefore be flexible to interpretation:

- ensuring that AI is used safely
- ensuring that AI is technically secure and functions as designed
- making sure that AI is appropriately transparent and explainable. There must be adequate assurance, not about the collection and use of big data but in particular about use of AI and algorithms. They must be transparent and explainable, precisely because of the likelihood of autonomous behaviour
- embedding considerations of fairness into AI
- defining legal persons' responsibility for AI governance
- clarifying routes to redress or contestability.

Even in the light of the *Policy Paper* and *Action Plan*, the subsequent AI Governance White Paper, *A Pro-innovation Approach to AI Regulation* in 2023[268] was a disappointment. The UK, perhaps to show its post Brexit independence from the EU, opted to approach technology with a much less comprehensive prescriptive legislative approach – 'pro-innovation' and 'context-specific' – which distributes responsibility for embedding ethical operation into AI systems across several UK sector regulators without giving them any new regulatory powers.

The 'context-specific approach' proposed that the cross-sectoral and overarching principles would be interpreted and implemented by regulators within the context of the environment they oversee and would therefore be flexible to interpretation. This may at some stage in the future develop into regulation, but in the short term it involves regulators in different sectors encouraging those they regulate to put into practice ethical principles for AI development and adoption but no oversight in sectors where there is no relevant regulator. There is no stated lead regulator and the various regulators are expected to interpret and apply the principles in their individual sectors in the expectation that they will somehow join the dots between them. They will have no new enforcement powers. There may be standards for developers and adopters but no obligation to adopt them.

The question as ever is whether this is adequate and whether the necessary objectives of achieving trustworthy AI and harmonised international standards are going to be achieved through the actions being taken in the

UK so far. Much of the White Paper's diagnosis was correct in terms of the risks and opportunities of AI. It emphasises the need for public trust and sets out the attendant risks, and adopts a realistic approach to the definition of AI. It made the case for central coordination and even admitted that this is what business has asked for, but the actual governance prescription in our view falls far short of what is required.

There is no recognition that the different forms of AI are technologies that need a comprehensive cross-sectoral approach to ensure that they are transparent, explainable, accurate, and free of bias, whether they are in an existing regulated or unregulated sector. Business needs a clear central oversight and compliance mechanism, not a patchwork of regulation. It is clear that the government's proposals will not meet its objective of ensuring public trust in AI technology.

This perception underlies the Ada Lovelace Institute paper of July 2023 *Regulating AI in the UK: Strengthening the UK's proposals for the benefit of people and society.*[269] As they say:

> *'Regulating AI' means addressing issues that could harm public trust in AI and the institutions using them, such as data-driven or algorithmic social scoring, biometric identification and the use of AI systems in law enforcement, education and employment.*

An approach that adopts divergent regulatory requirements across sectors runs the risk of creating barriers for developers and adopters having to navigate through the regulators of multiple sectors. Where a cross-compatible AI system is concerned – for example, in finance and telecoms – they would have to potentially understand and comply with different regimes administered by the FCA, Prudential Reg Authority, and Ofcom, all at the same time.

The author's conclusion is that the UK government's current proposals for the governance of AI are incomplete and unsatisfactory in a number of respects. Despite their commitment to trustworthy AI, and the clear evidence that there are legal gaps and risks to be mitigated here and now, the government seems determined to avoid any kind of overarching framework for regulation for the foreseeable future. However, in a surprising admission, the policy paper of 2022 did acknowledge that a context-driven approach may lead to less uniformity between regulators and could cause confusion and apprehension for stakeholders who will potentially need to consider a regime of multiple regulators.

As regards categorising AI rather than working to a clear definition of AI and determining what falls within scope – which is the approach taken by the EU AI Act and indeed the OECD whose definition the EU has adopted – the UK elected to follow an approach that instead sets out the core principles of AI and allows regulators to develop their own sector-specific definitions, 'to meet the evolving nature of AI as technology advances'. It stated that the overarching characteristics of 'adaptability' and 'autonomy' should be considered by all regulators as a means of determining the scope of their oversight.

It is clear from the White Paper and subsequent government statements that as yet there is no UK regulation proposed in terms of binding legal duties that would ensure that key ethical principles are observed. And this is so at a time when, as a result of media coverage of the capabilities of ChatGPT and GPT-4 and other large language models, interest in and apprehension about the impact of AI has never been higher. Indeed, the White Paper was doubly disappointing given that, in the month of its publication, the open letter we mention in Chapter 1 was published, in which over a thousand leading technologists pointed out the 'profound risks to society and humanity' of AI systems with human-competitive intelligence and called inter alia for AI developers to 'work with policymakers to dramatically accelerate development of robust AI governance systems'.

Some aspects of the operation of AI systems are covered by existing UK equalities and data protection legislation, but other principles are not, particularly in terms of accountability, transparency, explainability and right to redress. It is clear that some horizontality across government, business, and society is needed to embed the OECD principles.

We may not need to adopt as comprehensive an approach as the EU Artificial Intelligence Act, in terms of setting out a full risk hierarchy, but we need to accept the fact that AI is really very different to previous technology, given its potential black box and autonomous nature and the risks described in Chapters 2 and 3. Without a broad definition and without some overarching duty to carry out risk and impact assessment and subsequent regular audit to assess whether an AI system is conforming to AI principles, our governance of AI systems will be deficient. In addition, except for certain specific products such as driverless cars, no clear accountability or liability regime has been established for the operation of AI systems.

In this light, even by its own standards, the government's current proposals for a context-specific approach are inadequate. Vague 'AI guiding principles' and making existing regulators responsible for upholding them will fail to create trust and clarity for businesses, consumers, and investors. Instead, regulation should take the form of an overarching regulatory regime designed to ensure public transparency in the use of AI technologies and recourse across sectors for non-ethical use.

What is needed, is an approach which the recent interim report of the Science, Innovation and Technology Committee recommended in its inquiry into AI governance,[270] a combination of risk-based cross-sectoral regulation and specific regulation in sectors such as financial services, underpinned by common trustworthy standards of risk assessment, audit, and monitoring.

A report in June 2023, *An Ethical AI Future: Guardrails and Catalysts to Make Artificial Intelligence a Force for Good* by Policy Connect and the[271] All-Party Parliamentary Group on Data Analytics (APPGDA) likewise reviewed the government's White Paper. It agreed with its analysis of the risks and opportunities to the UK from new forms of AI but it also agreed with the Science and Technology Committee that harnessing the opportunities needs proper regulation and governance and it stated that industry needs an unambiguous and responsive regulatory environment to foster growth and innovation.

But it went further in setting out a number of practical measures to achieve a regulatory and governance environment designed to embed the principles set out in the White Paper. This included recommending that the government should introduce statutory duties, worded such as to require organisations to achieve the objective of 'doing no harm'. This could be tied into the design and bringing to market of 'high-risk' AI systems together with a requirement that the leadership team, at board level, should include a person accountable for ensuring due diligence on AI and ethics.

They also advocated a single independent, central body (which in the author's view could be the ICO) with strong regulatory authority, properly resourced, should be established in statute. The role would be to convene existing sector regulators, ensure AI principles are prioritised in their business plans and that their regulatory functions are properly resourced, proportionate, and agile and provide guidance to the public to help them guard against AI harms, alongside the establishment of single ombudsman.

We have world-beating AI researchers and developers. We need to support their international contribution, not fool them that they can operate in isolation. So it is clear, a much more horizontal cross-sectoral approach than the government is proposing is needed for the development and adoption of AI systems, one which sets out clear common duties to assess risk and impact and to adhere to common standards. Depending on the extent of the risk and impact assessed, further legal duties would arise.

In the middle of the debate about AI governance, we need to be clear that regulation is not necessarily the enemy of innovation; it can in fact be the stimulus and also be the key to gaining and retaining public trust around AI and its adoption, so that we can realise the benefits and minimise the risks.

As described in Chapter 4, this includes the public sector, where there is no central or local government compliance mechanism, no transparency yet in the form of a public register of use of automated decision-making and no recognition by government that explicit legislation and/or regulation for intrusive AI technologies – such as live facial recognition and other biometric capture – is needed.

A brighter spot for the future of AI and digital regulation in the UK is that, despite the lack of a firm regulatory framework, four key UK regulators – the ICO, Ofcom, CMA, and FCA – have created a Digital Regulation Cooperation Forum (DRCF) to pool expertise,[272] which will create some level of regulatory consistency in the digital area. This includes sharing expertise on sandboxing and drawing on input from a variety of expert institutes such as the Alan Turing Institute (ATI) in areas such as risk assessment, AI, audit, digital design frameworks and standards, digital advertising, and horizon scanning.

The explicit aims of the DRCF are:

- to promote greater coherence where regulatory regimes intersect
- to work collaboratively on areas of common interest
- to work together to build the necessary skills.

With the DRCF, these digital regulators are building common approaches to recruitment, graduates, attracting talent, early careers and outreach, and building digital regulation skills. These skills include algorithmic audit, data analytics, digital design frameworks, digital advertising, encryption, and horizon scanning.

The regulators need to go further, however. The Alan Turing Institute in their timely report *Common Regulatory Capacity for AI*[273] presents the results of research into how regulators can meet the challenge of regulating activities transformed by AI and can maximise the potential of AI for regulatory innovation.

They explore the capabilities required by the regulation of AI. Regulators need to be able to ensure that regulatory regimes are 'fit for AI'. They stress that it is essential to address AI-related risks and to maintain an environment that encourages innovation and the need for certainty about regulatory expectations, public trust in AI technologies, and the avoidance of undue regulatory obstacles.

They also emphasise the need to understand how to use AI itself for regulation. Regulatory bodies all face shared difficulties in making progress towards AI readiness. Common obstacles include limitations in knowledge and skills, insufficient coordination between regulators, issues of leadership and management of organisational and attitudinal change, and resource constraints.

The ATI believe that there is an urgent need for increased and sustainable forms of coordination on AI-related questions across the regulatory landscape. They agree that joined-up approaches to developing and sharing knowledge and resources can play a transformative role by enabling regulators to learn from each other and to increase their collective capacities in ways that leverage synergies and efficiencies.

The ATI also highlighted the need for access to new sources of shared AI expertise and proposed an AI and Regulation Common Capacity Hub which 'would have its home at a politically independent institution, established as a centre of excellence in AI, drawing on multidisciplinary knowledge and expertise from across the national and international research community.'

To our mind these recommendations themselves emphasise the need for the DRCF to take statutory form. It is also important that other regulators can come on board the DRCF, whether they are statutory or not. Even non-statutory regulators such as the Advertising Standards Authority could have a place at the table and join in benefitting from the digital centre of excellence being created.

Automated decision-making and the GDPR

One of the key issues in AI regulation is the extent to which there should be human oversight of decisions taken by AI systems that affect individuals based on the processing of their personal data by those systems. Currently, automated decision-making (ADM) is extensively used in decision-making around online advertising, employment outcomes, access to financial services, credit scoring, and the deployment and use of live facial recognition. Where important decisions are delegated to automated systems, there is an increased risk of discrimination, opacity, and lack of fairness from not accounting for individual circumstances and from not being able to explain decisions.

The advent of general-purpose AI systems like GPT-4 and Bard, and the use of 'plug-ins' that give them agency to interact with widely used systems means people are increasingly likely to be subject to ADM in new contexts.

One of the few areas specific to AI where there is existing law is as regards automated decision-making. Currently, Article 22 of UK GDPR (currently identical to the EU's provision) contains a general prohibition on fully automated decision-making that has a legal or 'similarly significant' effect on individuals – subject to limited exceptions. As a result, GDPR's Article 22 guarantees a human review of algorithms' decisions in areas as sensitive as loan provision or recruitment.[274]

However, a new bill before the UK parliament – the Data Protection and Digital Information Bill[275] – proposes to weaken protections against automated decision-making by replacing Article 22 of the UK GDPR with Articles that reduce human review of ADM. It proposes to remove the general prohibition as currently set out in UK GDPR and instead substitute conditions to be met for decisions involving special category data. The prohibition is replaced with a series of safeguards that must be in place. These measures include conditions such as enabling the data subject to make representations and obtain human intervention about automated decisions. The Bill also switches responsibility for ensuring that decisions by ADM are legal from the actor making the decision (usually an organisation) to a right that needs to be exercised by the affected individual. It takes decision-making on key terminology such as 'similarly significant' and 'meaningful human involvement' out of the hands of the Information Commissioner (the ICO).

Increasingly, however – and after all this is one of the OECD's AI principles – there is a public expectation that AI systems should be transparent and made 'explainable', to ensure accountability and leave room for automated decision-making to consider individual differences in circumstances. As mentioned earlier, The Science and Technology Select Committee report *Algorithms in Decision-Making* of May 2018[276] made extensive recommendations in this respect. It urged the adoption of a legally enforceable 'right to explanation' that allows citizens to find out how machine-learning programs reach decisions affecting them – and potentially challenge their results. It also called for algorithms to be added to a ministerial brief, and for departments to publicly declare where and how they use them.

Subsequently the UK Equalities and Human Rights Commission, in their advice on the new bill,[277] have recommended retaining Article 22 of

UK GDPR and extending the definition of automated decision-making to cover significantly or materially, as well as solely, automated processes. They also recommend maintaining explicit inclusion of profiling in the definition of a 'significant decision' in Article 22 UK GDPR. They say:

We are concerned that the proposed changes do not offer sufficient safeguards to protect individuals from unfair or discriminatory outcomes of automated decision-making. Data used to help AI-based tools to make decisions may contain biases, or the design of algorithms may reflect biases. This could lead to potential discriminatory automated decision-making.

The author agrees and believes not only that the UK should remain broadly aligned with the EU in terms of safeguards provided under the GDPR, but that in fact its reach should be strengthened so that it applies to partly automated processing as well, i.e. where it plays a significant part in decision-making.

There should be the right to an explanation of automated systems, where AI is only one part of the final decision in certain key circumstances, for instance where policing, justice, health, or personal welfare or finance is concerned. Citizens must be allowed to request information about algorithmic decisions which affect them and the data that is subject to decisions made.

As well as providing for fundamental principles of transparency and explainability, the Bill should strengthen human review of ADM and give rights to all decision subjects in recognition of the impact of ADM, not just the data source. The Bill should give rights to the people affected by an automated decision (decision subjects), not just those who provide data (data subjects).

A decision made about you may be determined by data about other people you have never met. The work of the UK exam regulator – the Office of Qualifications and Examinations Regulation (Ofqual) – in using the distribution of past exam results for its GCSE and A-level grading decisions during COVID-19 referred to earlier was a good example. Regulating decisions made about people solely on the basis of data held about them will have limited, even counter-productive, effects.

The author believes that the Bill should also enable representative organisations – such as unions or consumer rights bodies – to make complaints on behalf of data and/or decision subjects and provide opportunities for redress.

The role of international standards

Furthermore, despite the Communiqué agreed at the Bletchley Park AI Safety Summit, the UK government seemingly does not recognise the need for our developers to be confident that they can exploit their technology internationally.

In practice, our developers and adopters risk being forced to look over their shoulder at other more rigorous jurisdictions. If they have any international ambitions, they will have to conform to EU requirements under the forthcoming AI Act. In due course no doubt, they will also need to ensure that they avoid legal liability in the US by adopting generally accepted AI risk management standards such as those set by NIST.

If we can converge internationally, this would be a huge step towards the ethical development of AI and the ability of our tech community to develop with certainty. There is therefore an important question about the degree of harmonisation needed in order to ensure the most beneficial context for UK AI development and adoption. How can we ensure that, despite differing regulatory regimes, developers are able to commercialise their products on a global basis?

The answer in view lies in international agreement on common standards such as those of risk and impact assessment to be adopted for AI systems which incorporate what have become common internationally accepted AI ethics. Having a harmonised approach to standards would help provide the certainty that businesses need to develop and invest in the UK more readily, irrespective of the level of obligation to adopt them in different jurisdictions.

In this respect, the UK has the opportunity to play a much more positive role. Until recently the UK government, unlike its tech community, did not devote nearly enough attention to positive collaboration in a number of international AI forums such as the Council of Europe, UNESCO, and the OECD. It did, however, play an active part in the French and Canadian initiative, the Global Partnership on AI.[278] This was set up to 'support and guide the responsible development of artificial intelligence that is grounded in human rights, inclusion, diversity, innovation, and economic growth'. It has delivered some useful output, particularly in respect of AI and the future of work and the workplace.

The UK's AI Policy paper of 2022 led to the launch in October 2022 of the interactive AI Standards Hub,[279] led by the Alan Turing Institute with the support of the British Standards Institution and the National Physical Laboratory, designed to provide users across industry, academia, and regulators with practical tools and educational materials to effectively use and shape AI technical standards.

The Hub's mission is to advance trustworthy and responsible AI with a focus on the role that standards can play as governance tools and innovation mechanisms, and its work is structured around four pillars:

- **Observatory**: multiple interactive libraries that function as an observatory for AI standardisation and related developments in the UK and around the world.
- **Community and collaboration**: workshops and other live events, alongside online discussion forums and other interactive website features.
- **Knowledge and training**: e-learning materials and in-person training events aimed to equip stakeholders to actively contribute to the development of standards and to use and interpret standards that have been published.
- **Research and analysis**: research and analysis on strategic questions related to AI standardisation.

This in turn could lead to agreement on AI standards internationally which can be adopted, whether or not mandated by national regulation. Given the UK's strength in standards it could and should be at the heart of work advocating common elements of governance and regulation across jurisdictions, as the APPGDA report referred to earlier said.[280]

These are in the course of development by a range of bodies such as ISO,

NIST, CEN-CENELEC (the EU's standards setting bodies), the IEEE, and the UK's British Standards Institution.

There are already existing standards such as ISO/IEC 42001 Management Standard which provides guidelines for the governance and management of AI technologies, the Risk Management Framework developed by NIST, IEEE's 7000™-2021 ethical design standard, and many others which can be deployed.[281]

These, for example, can include standards for:

- ethically aligned design
- risk and impact assessment
- training and testing standards
- auditing and monitoring standards
- consumer assurance through Kitemarking.

We also have the example, developed by the Alan Turing Institute with the Council of Europe in 2022, of the Human Rights, Democracy, and the Rule of Law Impact Assessment – HUDERIA – a means of assessing the impact of AI systems on human rights.[282]

The OECD ONE AI group of experts is heavily engaged in a project[283] to find common ground between the various standards, with a view to international agreement, initially with regard to AI risk management frameworks, but with the prospect of further work on other AI standards.

As an added bonus for international convergence, we are also seeing increasing convergence around classification of AI systems, also led by the OECD. What is now needed is stronger political will in the West, and more widely, to achieve a broader form of regulatory convergence.

Whether we need an international AI Ethics Convention and supporting watchdog to enforce standards and to ensure global compliance on tackling AI risks, in the author's view, is yet to be seen, given the proliferation of international organisations with an interest in AI governance and standard setting. It is even more questionable whether the template for that body should be the International Atomic Energy Agency (IAEA) as suggested by Sam Altman, CEO of OpenAI in his evidence to the US Senate, mentioned earlier in Chapter 1.[284]

Tackling Goliath: AI and competition

In his *Sprawl* trilogy comprising *Neuromancer*, *Count Zero*, and *Mona Lisa Overdrive*, published in the 1980s,[285] the celebrated science fiction author William Gibson, the inventor of the concept of the Matrix, conjures up a world of competing autonomous AI cloud systems which are inescapable and impact every aspect of human life.

This may have seemed fanciful then, and even recently when we thought that general-purpose AI or even AGI were still some way off, but now it seems prescient given the rapid development of large language models (LLMs) like ChatGPT with their ability to write computer code and emulate humans in delivering information. These require access to massive datasets, highly sophisticated semiconductors, huge computing power, and access to scarce AI developer skills. Already we are seeing the emergence of a limited number of generative AI providers. We have OpenAI (backed by the massive resources of Microsoft), Bard from Google, and Meta's LlaMA. Then we have the products from what are essentially start-up businesses, Stable Diffusion from Stability AI (with investment from Amazon), Claude from Anthropic AI, and Cohere, backed by Nvidia the semiconductor giant and by Oracle and Salesforce. Concentration is likely to increase as generative AI systems become multimodal in nature and demand even greater resources for their development.

During the years of development of internet technology, particularly this century, leading up to the emergence of these LLMs, and especially as regards search engines, cloud services, and social media applications, there has been a major concentration of internet platforms. The digital landscape is now dominated by the power of a limited number of big tech companies.

Just to provide some perspective on this, the so-called GAMMA companies – Google (Alphabet), Amazon, Microsoft, Meta, and Apple – have a combined market valuation of around $10 trillion which is over three times the UK's GDP in 2022.[286]

As the columnist Gerard Baker has noted, Apple, Alphabet, Amazon, Microsoft, Meta, Apple, with around 160,000 employees, made $170 billion in profit 2022 on revenues of about $390 billion – almost twice the total economic output of Ukraine, a country of 40 million people. As he says, 'The larger reality, becoming clearer by the year, is that they are now more powerful – and less accountable – than most governments in the world.'[287]

This has been partly due to Metcalfe's law of networks.[288] Network effects mean people benefit from being on the same platform as each other. The more people who join a platform, the better the platform is. But that effect then impedes people's ability to switch to new platforms when their user base is lower.

It is also partly due to predatory acquisitions of smaller businesses by the large tech platforms, which has drastically reduced competition over the medium and long term. Looking at the publicly disclosed acquisitions between 2008 and 2018, Google has acquired 168 companies, Facebook has acquired 71 companies, and Amazon has acquired 60 companies.[289]

Our greatest UK success stories tend to then be acquired by foreign companies – for example, Google's acquisition of DeepMind, Twitter's acquisition of Magic Pony, and Apple's acquisition of Shazam. As a result, UK innovation is subsumed into the US tech giants, and ultimately the UK does not realise the full economic benefit of that innovation.

In addition, both in the EU and here, one of the biggest issues is the power of Big Tech online, in terms of their market dominance in relation to access to data, and the impact on consumers of the way that their algorithms operate. Large platforms generate enormous amounts of data that they can use to better develop and target products and services to consumers, often using algorithms. But a lack of access to that data then becomes a barrier to entry for potential new entrants.

Lord Puttnam has rightly likened the power of the platforms to Big Oil or the railroads of the 19th century, and we need the same vigorous competition remedies to combat them. In the Lords AI Select Committee Report too they noted that access to large quantities of data is one of the factors fuelling the current AI boom. It was adamant that large companies which have control over vast quantities of data must be prevented from becoming overly powerful within the AI landscape.

The House of Lords Select Committee chaired by Lord Puttnam, in its report *Digital Technology and the Resurrection of Trust* in 2020 referred to earlier, was also mindful of the danger of a lack of media competition – the need for plurality of media outlets and opinion.

So on many counts the huge concentration of wealth, power, and data in a few US hyper-scalers is concerning, inhibiting investment and innovation. The imbalance of power and market share is a barrier to entry for start-ups, which struggle to compete against the tech giants and may also struggle to attract investment.

But it is clear that existing regulatory tools do not work well in digital markets and are not good at quickly identifying and addressing competition concerns which arise. Existing regulatory powers are primarily backwards-looking and can only tackle harms after they have occurred and can involve protracted court battles over long periods of time. Given the pace that these markets move at, that simply means it's too late; the problems and the damage have been already done by the time they can be resolved.

The *Unlocking Digital Competition* report of 2019 from the Digital Competition Expert Panel[290] chaired by Professor Jason Furman first started the debate in the UK about the enforcement powers of the Competition and Markets Authority (CMA) in the digital environment and proposed the setting up of a specialist unit which would drive a pro-competition digital regulatory regime that is able to shape firms' behaviour in advance with enforceable Codes of Conduct and other forms of pro-competition intervention.

In January 2021, the report by John Penrose MP *Power to the People*,[291] commissioned by the government, on how the UK's approach to competition and consumer issues could be improved identified the lack of speed in enforcement of competition law as a central issue, with the consequence that delay 'benefits big business over smaller businesses and entrepreneurial activity in the digital age' as a central policy concern.

After some considerable delay a new Digital Markets Unit[292] was set up in shadow form within the UK Competition and Markets Authority prior to being placed on a statutory basis. This would act as a centre of expertise for digital markets and in due course 'operationalise a new pro-competition regime for digital markets' particularly in respect of companies having 'Strategic Market Status' with the adoption of an enforceable code of conduct to tackle digital markets and financial penalties for non-compliance.

The regime would be 'unashamedly pro-competition', said the then Business Secretary Kwasi Kwarteng, adding that the pro-competition regime would 'help curb the dominance of the tech giants'.[293]

A Digital Markets Competition and Consumers and Consumer Competition Bill has now been introduced in the UK which will set up the new Digital Markets Unit (DMU) in statutory form and introduce a new 'pro-competition regime' for digital markets. The essence of the new provisions is to provide the competition regulator with tools designed to deliver fast, targeted action to make markets more contestable and to protect businesses and consumers from the effects of strategic market power in the short term.

The DMU will assess whether a firm holds both substantial and entrenched market power, or strategic market status through a nine-month investigation and the status will last for five years before being renewed. But given there will be a consumer benefits exemption it is important that short-term consumer welfare is not the sole or sometimes even the primary consideration in assessing whether competition is adequate.

The EU for its part has introduced the Digital Services Act and Digital Markets Act with similar intent.[294] The US Federal Trade Commission has also been asking the same questions rather robustly, both as regards harm and competition with court action commenced against Facebook.[295]

So we now have a realistic prospect internationally across both Europe and the US of an effective digital markets regime which will use 'ex-ante' regulation, whereby regulators aim to identify problems beforehand and shape market behaviour through clear requirements which seek to manage the harmful effects of substantial and entrenched market power, by setting out how big tech firms are expected to behave, thus protecting consumers and competing businesses.

In the UK it is hoped that the CMA's approach to the Microsoft acquisition of Activision Blizzard[296] and Ofcom's decision to refer the hyper-scalers in cloud services for an investigation by the CMA[297] heralds an appetite to tackle future concentration among the generative AI developers.

The UK's Competition and Markets Authority's initiative in conducting a review and completing an initial report of the competition and consumer protection principles that should best guide the ongoing development of AI foundation models and their use is another welcome sign of this appetite.[298] The initial report recommends that the key overarching principles to guide the development and deployment of Foundation Models should be:

- **Access**: Ongoing access to key inputs.
- **Diversity**: Sustained diversity of business models, including both open and closed.
- **Choice**: Sufficient choice for businesses so they can decide how to use Foundation Models.
- **Flexibility**: Flexibility to switch or use multiple Foundation Models according to need.
- **Fair Dealing**: No anti-competitive self-preferencing, tying or bundling.
- **Transparency**: Consumers and businesses are given information about the risks and limitations of content generated by Foundation Models so they can make informed choices.

This determination to engage in active oversight bodes well for when the new pro-competition powers for the CMA come into effect. Whether this will be enough to buck the trend towards concentration experienced in other digital fields must, however, be an open question at this stage.

We may well need to go further than currently envisaged. The Open Markets Institute comprehensively examines the AI competitive landscape in its November 2023 paper *AI in the Public Interest: Confronting the Monopoly Threat*.[299]

The report unpacks the already extreme levels of concentration in AI and advocates for the use of competition policy and other tools to ensure that AI works in the public interest. In their words it highlights how '*just a handful of dominant tech companies – by exploiting their existing dominance and aggressively co-opting other actors – have already positioned themselves to control the future of artificial intelligence and magnify many of the worst problems of the digital age.*'

The report explores in detail how AI concentration is set to worsen these problems and proposes a number of immediate actions to tackle monopoly power in AI, including:

- Banning all discrimination by powerful digital gatekeepers in the delivery of essential services to individuals and businesses.
- Recognising cloud computing as an essential infrastructure, separating ownership and control from the largest gatekeeper platforms, and regulating it as a public utility.
- Reversing gatekeeper efforts to control AI development through mergers, investments, and partnerships, and blocking similar deals in future.
- Recognising that any data collected by large platforms in their capacities as essential services is public in nature, and establishing a public-interest regime to govern access.
- Aggressively enforcing copyright laws to protect the properties of authors, creators, and other independent publishers from misappropriation and misuse by gatekeeper corporations.

The diagnosis is clear. The question is whether we have the political will to deliver the prescription.

9 AI the Global Opportunity: Race or Regulation?

The climate of Sino-British relationships has changed greatly in recent years. For most of the past 20 years in Europe and to some extent in the US there has been a great emphasis on moving the relationship forward in investment and trade, in the hope – at least by the business community –that China's economic reform and opening up policies started by Deng Xiaoping in 1979 would lead to a more rules-based approach as well as to societal change.

China described its relations with Britain during the Cameron premiership as going through a 'golden era'. All the talk was of 'Win Win' investment and of Britain being an important destination for Belt and Road collaboration. As recently as 2015, the UK became the first G7 member to sign up to China's new competitor to the World Bank, the Asian Infrastructure Investment Bank.[300] As a consequence, the level of investment by Chinese investors grew exponentially. It stands at over £135bn, invested in critical infrastructure, property, and shares in FTSE 100 companies.[301] China is the UK's largest import market and sixth-largest export partner for goods.[302]

The UK–China relationship was in marked contrast to the US approach which, under President Obama, developed a much less user-friendly approach to Chinese investment.

This was in large part as a result of its perception of China's increasing strength in technology. The growing importance of China's tech industries has been all too apparent in the last decade. It is clear that platforms such as Baidu, Alibaba, Alipay, Tencent, and TikTok – and Huawei in mobile communications and wifi – rival anything the West has to offer. There is no doubt that China is already among the most advanced countries in AI – indeed a leader in some AI tech. China's State Council in 2017 issued the *New Generation Artificial Intelligence Development Plan*[303] which seeks to build an AI industry worth nearly US$150bn to make China 'the world's primary AI innovation centre' by 2030. China is also making massive strides in other areas such as cryptography, 5G electric vehicles, and genomics –

not forgetting China's desire for supremacy in quantum computing. US investment, taken as a whole, is ahead on total R&D spending, but China is well ahead of the EU. And in terms of supercomputers it is well ahead of both.[304]

Concern is compounded over the use to which applications such as facial recognition and emotion AI are being put, as forms of society control within China in general, and in Xinjiang in particular. Indeed, the prevailing view is that Xinjiang is used as a test bed for surveillance technology linked to Chinese companies – particularly Huawei, Hikvision, Dahua, and ZTE. They then via the Belt and Road Initiative – which finances overseas infrastructure – supply AI surveillance technology to participating countries.

The Belt and Road Initiative itself is increasingly seen as an aggressive China forward policy rather than the use of soft power. There is also great Western suspicion that China is using its membership of global standards setting bodies such as the International Telecommunications Union and United Nations Industrial Development Organisation to further its own competitive ambitions.[305]

As a result, Huawei found itself blocked from US government contracts and barred from making acquisitions through the US Committee on Foreign Investment (CFIUS) process in attempting to buy 3Com, a maker of anti-hacking computer software as early as 2008, and later, in 2011, from acquiring 3Leaf, the cloud technology firm.[306]

President Biden proved to be as hard-line over security issues and relations with China as his predecessor President Trump. At the Carbis Bay Summit in June 2021 he pressed other G7 members to take a tougher line on China and show greater commitment to his infrastructure alternative to the Belt and Road Initiative, the 'Build Back Better World Partnership' (B3W) which significantly included digital technology.[307,308]

Even so, the Biden and previous administrations have been criticised for not organising and investing to win the technology competition against what is described as 'a committed competitor'. The Final Report of the National Security Commission on Artificial Intelligence chaired by Eric Schmidt, the former CEO of Google, described AI competition with China as a 'national emergency', asserting that China could replace the US as an AI superpower.[309]

In response, the US approach has in recent times been to place a ban on the export of semiconductors to China and to place investment controls on technology that aids surveillance and repression. In turn, China is retaliating, using the supply of rare earth minerals, important in the manufacture of many digital devices, as a counter. It has imposed export controls on technology such as 3D printing, drones, and voice recognition.

If both the Trump and Biden administrations have tended to view AI through the lens of a technology race with China, the same is true of Congress. The US Innovation and Competition Act – which eventually became the CHIPS and Science Act[310] – was designed to boost US investment in basic and advanced research, commercialisation, and education and training programs in artificial intelligence, semiconductors, quantum computing, advanced communications, biotechnology, and advanced energy. With bipartisan support, it moved through the Senate at an unusually swift pace when it started on its legislative journey. Proponents of that legislation made clear throughout that their motive was to counter China's ascendancy in transformative innovations like AI, superconductors, and robotics.

In consequence in recent years, in countries allied to the US, the geopolitical climate towards China and Chinese technology has cooled, for example in the UK, many parts of Europe, Australia, and India – with Italy withdrawing from Belt and Road membership, China's flagship diplomatic initiative.

The cooling effect is partly a result of China being seen as eroding the rule of law in Hong Kong through new security laws and human rights violation in Xinjiang but, also to a mounting degree, shared concerns with the US over security threats from Chinese digital technology and cyberspace activity.

The warning signals were first set off by China's adoption in 2015 of its Made in China 2025 policy,[311] which set out 10 sectors – such as robotics, semiconductors, and advanced medical technology – in which domestic companies were expected to dominate in the Chinese market and compete globally. This has led to increased concern over the appropriation by Chinese companies of Western know-how and intellectual property in tech development.

Having diverged for a decade, driven by the prospect of loosened intelligence ties, the UK – along with others such as Australia – has changed course to align itself much more closely with the China policy of successive US administrations.

The UK now has its own legislation – the National Security and Investment Act (NSIA),[312] which set up a review process designed to do a similar job to CFIUS – the Committee on Foreign Investment, in the US – charged with screening inward investment. The NSIA identifies 17 'sensitive sectors' where notification to, and approval from, a new Investment Security Unit will be required, which includes advanced robotics, artificial intelligence, computing hardware and quantum technologies. Accordingly, the Secretary of State for Business, Energy, and Industrial Strategy will have the power to prohibit or reverse certain transactions which they believe pose a national security risk or to impose conditions to the transactions.

Furthermore, after the progressive hardening of policy, we have also seen the passage of telecommunications security legislation to ensure that equipment provided by telecoms suppliers deemed 'high risk' – in other words Huawei – are removed from our 4G and 5G infrastructure by 2027 and a 5G diversification strategy for telecoms networks is being put in place.[313]

An even clearer indication of a change of government policy towards China is the Integrated Review of Security Defence Development and Foreign Policy set out in Global Britain in a Competitive Age published in March 2021.[314] Among other things, this describes the context as defined by:

geopolitical and geoeconomic shifts such as China's increasing power and assertiveness, internationally systemic competition, including between states, and between democratic and authoritarian values as well as systems of government and rapid technological change.

China is regarded as a systemic competitor whereas Russia is described as a threat.

At the heart of this competition is AI and other tech research and development. Technological competition is the new battleground. Consequently, in recent years, the head of MI5, Ken McCallum; the former head of MI6, Sir Alex Younger; and the former Director General of GCHQ, Sir Jeremy Fleming, have warned of the cyber, technological, and scientific dangers posed by Chinese competition and actions in terms variously of cybersecurity, quantum computing, the design and freedom of the internet, and the security of emerging technologies such as smart cities.[315]

The creation of the National Cyber Security Centre back in 2016[316] and more recently the Advanced Research and Invention Agency (ARIA)[317] and the creation of the new Department for Science, Innovation and Technology subsuming the Office for Science and Technology Strategy (OSTS) has been part of the UK's response to this technological and cybersecurity challenge.

There is also pressure – partly as a result of experience during the COVID pandemic of PPE procurement issue – to reduce supply chain dependence on China. The White House has recently produced a set of reports entitled *Building Resilient Supply Chains, Revitalising Manufacturing and Fostering Broad-based Growth.*[318] They cover semiconductor manufacturing; large-capacity batteries, such as those for electric vehicles; critical minerals and materials; as well as pharmaceuticals and advanced pharmaceutical ingredients.

Nowhere has had a more sudden change of approach to China than the EU. In December 2020, Ursula Von Der Leyen, the President of the Commission, hailed the new Comprehensive Agreement on Investment as 'a values based trade agenda', when it was clearly thought that trade with China and geopolitics could be separated.[319] Six months later the emphasis was on President Xi's 'authoritarian shift', with the European Parliament in the face of the retaliatory sanctions by China on EU diplomats, members of the European Parliament and academics working at European think-tanks voting against the deal so bringing the EU much closer into alignment with the US.[320]

The EU Commission has argued for the concept of 'digital sovereignty' designed to reduce its dependence on foreign technology – both US and Chinese – and to increase its competitiveness. European Commission President Ursula von der Leyen and Josep Borrell, the EU foreign policy chief, indicated the Commission's shift in approach in a letter to leaders of the EU member states in April 2021:

The reality is that the EU and China have fundamental divergences, be it about their economic systems and managing globalization, democracy and human rights, or on how to deal with third countries. These differences are set to remain for the foreseeable future and must not be brushed under the carpet.[321]

A group of legislators from the G7 put what they see as the technology imperative more starkly in a letter to their heads of government in January 2021:

The platform technologies of quantum computing, artificial intelligence, and 5G deployment are set to radically change our global economy over the coming decades. The power inherent in these technologies cannot be overstated. While these technologies have the potential to improve the lives of citizens across the globe, they must be developed around core principles that safeguard user data. The PRC has taken the lead in developing some of these future industries – at times to the detriment of other nations through unfair or even illegal means. The Free World must avoid becoming dependent on a country that rejects market principles and democratic values. A coordinated partnership amongst our countries to lead the development of these technologies and set global norms and standards for their use is thus essential to make full use of their potential without compromising our security and interests.[322]

It is now clear that the West and China are potentially in a major struggle for technological supremacy. Western industrial policies are reflecting this. Internationally the strategic response of the West has been to create the Global Partnership on AI, mentioned earlier, initially a Franco/Canadian initiative, supported by the G7 and OECD, to: 'support the responsible and human-centric development and use of AI in a manner consistent with human rights, fundamental freedoms, and our shared democratic values'.

But the question remains whether even in the face of this we can reach global agreement on the risks posed by AI and need for ethical governance. The EU Commissioner responsible for Digital, Margrethe Verstager, the Executive Vice-President of the European Commission for 'A Europe Fit for the Digital Age', and former Competition Commissioner, said at the CogX Festival in 2021, 'we [the EU] need an alliance of democracies to underpin the values in our technology.'[323] But we need to go further than this.

If we are to meet the challenges posed internationally by AI in its increasingly sophisticated form, we need to develop a common approach to its governance, at the very least regarding AI safety, beyond the democratic world.

Professor Luciano Floridi, Founding Director of the Digital Ethics Center at Yale, states that traditional analogue sovereignty, as he calls it, which controls territory, resources, and people is now insufficient. It must also reach an accommodation with digital power, which controls data, software, standards, and protocols and is mostly in the hands of global tech companies. As he says, there needs to be a supranational element to digital sovereignty for it to be effective.[324]

Despite the constraints, we need to be outward-looking. It is one thing to assert our values and desire to be competitive, it is quite another to adopt a consistently hostile stance to cooperation with China on the safety and ethics of new technology. Whether we are optimists or pessimists about future relations with China we need to continue to engage in this field.

In 2019, shortly after signing up at the G20 meeting to the G20 AI principles, the Beijing Academy of Artificial Intelligence (BAAI), an organisation backed by the Chinese Ministry of Science and Technology (MOST) and the Beijing Municipal Government, released the *Beijing AI Principles*, an outline to guide the research and development, implementation, and governance of AI, based on these principles.[325]

Subsequently Matt Sheehan of the Carnegie Endowment for International Peace in early 2022 wrote a paper entitled *China's New AI Governance Initiatives Shouldn't Be Ignored*.[326] In it he points to the emergence of three different approaches to AI governance, each championed by a different branch of the Chinese bureaucracy, and each at a different level of maturity.

These comprise the Cyberspace Administration of China (CAC), the Chinese national internet regulator, which is focused on rules for online algorithms, with a focus on public opinion; the China Academy of Information and Communications Technology (CAICT) focused on tools for testing and certification of 'trustworthy AI' systems; and MOST, which is focused on establishing AI ethics principles and creating tech ethics review boards within companies and research institutions.

He describes how the CAC made headlines in August 2021 when it released a draft set of 30 rules for regulating internet recommendation algorithms and soon after a three-year roadmap for governing all internet algorithms.[327] In July 2021, the CAICT released the country's first White Paper on trustworthy AI. As Sheehan comments, 'The way the CAICT defines trustworthy AI in its core principles looks very similar to the definitions that have come out of US and European institutions.' In December 2022, the CAC issued regulations prohibiting the creation and distribution of AI-generated content without clear labelling, such as watermarks.[328]

And then in August 2023 the *Generative AI Measure*[329] was introduced by the CAC for the regulation of generative AI training data. This will apply to domestic Chinese companies and to overseas generative AI service providers offering generative AI services to the general public in China and have been described as among some of the most 'stringent and detailed globally'.

Recently, the Deputy Prime minister, Oliver Dowden, ahead of the Global AI Safety Summit held at Bletchley Park, defended the government's decision to invite China to the summit, saying that the West could not go it alone in an attempt to set the ground rules for AI and had no choice but to operate in tandem with China, even if it did not share the same values.[330]

He said that the technology 'will require us to work with countries that do not always share our values' and added: 'AI is coming whether we like it or not, and it will be beyond the ability of any one country to control or regulate it.'

In the event, China attended the summit, and signed up to the *Bletchley Declaration* alongside the United States, 26 other countries, and the EU. As discussed previously, it is not sufficient, but it had the important aim of boosting global efforts to cooperate on AI safety. Even those sceptical of developing relationships with China should, in the author's view, welcome this and promote further cooperation on AI standards.

10 Concluding Thoughts for a Technological Tomorrow

There are many opportunities that AI presents, to transform many aspects of people's lives for the better, from healthcare and scientific research to the daily commute, in education, in agriculture, and in meeting many of the sustainable development goals. In addition to the overarching regulatory issues, each sector undoubtedly brings its own particular regulatory challenges.

In the foregoing chapters the many challenges posed by AI have been set out, together with some practical solutions. These included some of the risks posed by AI, especially in the public sector, of reflecting and exacerbating social prejudices and bias, undermining the right to privacy, such as through the use of live facial recognition technology. Also highlighted has been the threat of AI spreading misinformation and disinformation, the so-called hallucinations of large language models, and the creation of deepfakes and hyper-realistic sexual abuse.

The consequent need for skilling and upskilling has also been highlighted. We must have an approach to AI that augments jobs as far as possible and equips people with the skills they need – whether to use new technology or to create it – while also attracting and welcoming the best talent from around the world. We should go further on Lifelong Learning. A massive skills and upskilling agenda is needed, and much greater diversity and inclusion in the AI workforce.

Concentrations of power that stifle competition, limit choice for consumers, and hamper progress need to be effectively countered.

In particular, the author has advocated the need, as far as possible, to ensure international convergence and interoperability of standards for AI systems.

As regards the creative industries, there are clearly great opportunities in relation to the use of AI, and many sectors are already using the technology in a variety of different ways to enhance their creativity and make it easier for the public to discover new content. But there are also challenges, major questions over authorship and infringement of intellectual property, and the view of large language model developers that they do not need to seek permission to ingest content to train and operate their systems.

Then there are the issues relating to performing rights, the faking of actors', musicians', artists' and other creators' images, voices, likenesses, styles, and attributes. We need to ensure that creators and artists are sufficiently protected.

This book has only scratched the surface in tackling AI governance issues but it is hoped that those who read it will build on some of the practical ideas and steps put forward.

In particular, given the pressures of parliamentary and professional life, the author has not been able to cover sectoral issues in any detail in these chapters. There are certain sectors, however, that are a priority for early specific exploration given AI's potential impact on them.

AI in education is a prime candidate. AI used appropriately and ethically promises to play a key role in addressing a number of entrenched challenges in education provision, reducing the burdens placed on overworked teachers, allowing education systems to move beyond focusing on a narrow range of skills and facilitate high-quality provision at scale. AI could also be central to the design of high-calibre lifelong education systems. That's why there is great significance in the work of the Institute for Ethical AI in Education (IEAIED) created in 2018 by Professor Rose Luckin, the director of EDUCATE Ventures; Sir Anthony Seldon, the former vice-chancellor of the University of Buckingham; and Priya Lakhani, the founder and CEO of Century Tech, and Sir Anthony's new initiative AI in Education. The IEAIED's Ethical AI in education framework has lasting value in outlining the principles and the actions that educational institutions should adopt in the use and procurement of AI-based education technology and we now need to start building effective AI in education governance, incorporating those principles.[331]

Specific regulation for AI systems is another aspect that healthcare AI developers and adopters too will need to factor in, going forward. The greater the impact on the patient that an AI application has, the stronger the need for clear and continuing ethical governance to ensure trust in its use, including preventing potential bias, ensuring explainability, accuracy, privacy, cybersecurity, and reliability, and determining how much human oversight should be maintained. This becomes of even greater importance in the long term, if AI systems in healthcare become more autonomous.

In particular, AI in healthcare will not be successfully deployed unless the public is confident that its health data will be used in an ethical manner, is of high quality, assigned its true value, and used for the greater benefit of UK healthcare. The Ada Lovelace Institute in conjunction with the NHS AI Lab, for example,[332] has led the way in developing an algorithmic impact assessment for data access in a healthcare environment which demonstrates the crucial risk and ethical factors that need to be considered in the context of AI development and adoption in this context.

Nor has the long-standing suggestion of a Hippocratic oath for AI developers been explored, although it has attractions.[333] Also the question of how we develop a cadre of professionals with the skills to independently give assurance about the adherence to standards of AI systems, although many would regard members of the IAPP – the International Association of Privacy Professionals – as strong candidates[334]

At the conclusion of the UK's AI Safety Summit at Bletchley Park in 2023, the closing Communiqué[335] rightly identified the full range of present and future risks and protection of human rights, transparency and the need to address issues of explainability, fairness, accountability, regulation, safety, appropriate human oversight, ethics, bias mitigation, privacy, and data protection. The Communiqué talked of encouraging 'all relevant actors to provide context-appropriate transparency and accountability on their plans to measure, monitor and mitigate potentially harmful capabilities and the associated effects that may emerge.'

A better outcome in our view would have been agreement that, here and now, we need to work towards common international standards for ethical design, risk assessment, testing, and audit of AI systems. Given that there is no agreement on how far to make these mandatory through regulation or legislation we needed a commitment to interoperability and convergence of these standards.

As an optimist, the author believes that new technology can lead potentially to greater productivity and more efficient use of resources generally, but as stated earlier, we should be clear about its purpose and implications when we adopt it. As emphasised in Chapter 8, we need to be clear that regulation is not necessarily the enemy of innovation, and the need for public trust and trustworthy AI should be reflected in how we regulate.

As noted earlier, 2024 is a record year for elections across the globe, with over 2 billion people going to the polls. With fresh electoral mandates we hope that governments across the world will seize the AI regulatory agenda and identify the key areas for action, such as the legal gap where a duty of explainability and transparency or accountability should lie, or where there should be greater protection of intellectual property or more effective prevention of misinformation and deepfakes.

That combined with internationally agreed standards for AI systems would, we believe, provide the necessary certainty and confidence for citizens and businesses alike in the beneficial development of AI going forward.

As we do go forward, however, it is worth remembering that humans have met the challenges of change effectively before. After all, it was Heraclitus, the ancient Greek philosopher, some 2500 years ago, who observed that 'change alone is unchanging'.[336] Brad Smith and Carole Ann Browne point the way to the appropriate response at the conclusion of *Tools and Weapons*:[337] '*Technology innovation is not going to slow down. The work to manage it needs to speed up.*' We all need to take that to heart.

Postscript

At the time of this book going to press the UK Government published its response to the AI Regulation White Paper consultation. Despite evidence of current risks, and in particular those posed by general purpose AI impacting on a range of sectors, the approach continues to be essentially voluntary and sector specific, added to a lack of leadership on intellectual property rights. This patchwork approach makes the need for convergence on international standards of continuing relevance and importance.

ENDNOTES

[1] Yuval Noah Harari argues that AI has hacked the operating system of human civilisation, *The Economist* April 2023: https://www.economist.com/by-invitation/2023/04/28/yuval-noah-harari-argues-that-ai-has-hacked-the-operating-system-of-human-civilisation?utm_content=section_content&gad_source=1&gclid=CjwKCAiAqY6tBhAtEiwAHeRopV6eX00WurCW9qlwcwh9Efof-glVeorJacNHoDinlKrExqoLyB9xxhoC62UQAvD_BwE&gclsrc=aw.ds

[2] Future of Life Open Letter, 22 March 2023: https://futureoflife.org/open-letter/pause-giant-ai-experiments/

[3] National AI Strategy, HM Government, September 2021: Command Paper 525 https://assets.publishing.service.gov.uk/media/614db4d1e90e077a2cbdf3c4/National_AI_Strategy_-_PDF_version.pdf

[4] *Mail Online*, 16 April 2018: https://www.dailymail.co.uk/news/article-5620553/Killer-robots-reality-peers-warn.html

[5] Stephen Hawking: AI will be 'either best or worst thing' for humanity, *Guardian* 19 October 2016: https://www.theguardian.com/science/2016/oct/19/stephen-hawking-ai-best-or-worst-thing-for-humanity-cambridge#

[6] BCS Open letter calls for AI to be recognised as 'force for good not threat to humanity': https://www.bcs.org/articles-opinion-and-research/bcs-open-letter-calls-for-ai-to-be-recognised-as-force-for-good-not-threat-to-humanity/

[7] Elon Musk and Others Call for Pause on A.I., Citing 'Profound Risks to Society': https://www.nytimes.com/2023/03/29/technology/ai-artificial-intelligence-musk-risks.html

[8] AI Poses 'Risk of Extinction', Industry Leaders Warn: https://www.nytimes.com/2023/05/30/technology/ai-threat-warning.html

[9] OpenAI's Sam Altman Urges A.I. Regulation in Senate Hearing: https://www.nytimes.com/2023/05/16/technology/openai-altman-artificial-intelligence-regulation.html#:~:text=But%20on%20Tuesday%2C%20Sam%20Altman,others%20like%20Google%20and%20Microsoft.

[10] Stephanie Hare: *Technology is Not Neutral, A Short Guide to Technology Ethics*, London Publishing Partnership, February 2022

[11] Cathy O'Neil: *Weapons of Math Destruction: How Big Data Increases Inequality and Threatens Democracy*, Penguin Books, September 2016

[12] Hannah Fry: *Hello World: How to be Human in the Age of the Machine*, Doubleday, September 2018

[13] How We Analyzed the COMPAS Recidivism Algorithm: by Jeff Larson, Surya Mattu, Lauren Kirchner and Julia Angwin, May 2016: https://www.propublica.org/article/how-we-analyzed-the-compas-recidivism-algorithm

[14] European Commission: Artificial Intelligence – Questions and Answers: https://ec.europa.eu/commission/presscorner/detail/en/QANDA_21_1683

[15] White House Fact Sheet October 2023: President Biden Issues Executive Order on Safe, Secure, and Trustworthy Artificial Intelligence: https://www.whitehouse.gov/briefing-room/statements-releases/2023/10/30/fact-sheet-president-biden-issues-executive-order-on-safe-secure-and-trustworthy-artificial-intelligence/

[16] G7 Digital and Tech Minister's Statement on the Hiroshima AI process, 7 September 2023: http://www.g8.utoronto.ca/ict/2023-statement.html

[17] https://www.whitehouse.gov/briefing-room/statements-releases/2023/12/06/g7-leaders-statement-6/#:~:text=The%20achievement%20of%20the%20Hiroshima,plan%20developed%20by%20relevant%20Ministers.

[18] Hiroshima Process International Guiding Principles for Organizations Developing and Hiroshima Process International Code of Conduct for Organizations Developing Advanced AI Systems: https://www.mofa.go.jp/ecm/ec/page5e_000076.html

[19] The Bletchley Declaration by Countries Attending the AI Safety Summit, 1–2 November 2023: https://www.gov.uk/government/publications/ai-safety-summit-2023-the-bletchley-declaration/the-bletchley-declaration-by-countries-attending-the-ai-safety-summit-1-2-november-2023

[20] *The Ancient Forerunner of AI*, Adrienne Mayor, Engelsberg Ideas 2023: https://engelsbergideas.com/notebook/the-ancient-forerunner-of-ai/ The Ancient Forerunner of AI and Gods and Robots: Myths, Machines, and Ancient Dreams of Technology. Princeton University Press, 2019

[21] Isaac Asimov, *I, Robot* stories. The stories originally appeared in the American magazines *Super Science Stories* and *Astounding Science Fiction* between 1940 and 1950 and were then collected into a 1950 publication.

[22] Ai-Da robot makes history by giving evidence to parliamentary inquiry, October 2022: https://www.independent.co.uk/news/uk/politics/house-of-lords-technology-liberal-democrat-b2200496.html

[23] Brian Christian, *The Alignment Problem – Machine Learning and Human Values*, WW Norton & Company, 2020 and Professor Stuart Russell, *Human Compatible: Artificial Intelligence and the Problem of Control*, Allen Lane, 2019

[24] Martin Rees, *On the Future: Prospects for Humanity*, Princeton University Press, September 2018

[25] House of Lords Special Inquiry into Risk Assessment and Risk Planning, Preparing for Extreme Risks: Building a Resilient Society, December 2021: https://committees. parliament.uk/committee/483/risk-assessment-and-risk-planning-committee/ publications/

[26] Select Committee on Risk Assessment and Risk Planning. Wednesday Corrected oral evidence for Wednesday 23 June 2021: https://committees.parliament.uk/oralevidence/ 2448/html/

[27] Select Committee on Risk Assessment and Risk Planning. Wednesday Corrected oral evidence for Wednesday 25 November 2020: https://committees.parliament.uk/ oralevidence/ 1295/html/

[28] Institute for Government, Managing Extreme Risks July 2022: https://www.institute forgovernment.org.uk/sites/default/files/publications/Managing-extreme-risks.pdf

[29] Oliver Letwin, *Apocalypse How?: Technology and the Threat of Disaster*, Atlantic Books, March 2020

[30] Elon Musk's refusal to have Starlink support Ukraine attack in Crimea raises questions for Pentagon: https://apnews.com/article/spacex-ukraine-starlink-russia-air-force-fde93d9a69d7dbd1326022ecfdbc53c2

[31] Risk Assessment and Risk Planning Committee Corrected oral evidence: Risk assessment and risk planning for Wednesday 26 May 2021: https://committees. parliament.uk/oralevidence/2282/html/

[32] https://www.townplanning.info/town-planning-in-england/development-plans/

[33] Andreas Klinke & Ortwin Renn, Forum for Qualitative Research, Vl 7 No 1 January 2006, Systemic Risks as Challenge for Policy Making in Risk Governance: https:// www.qualitative-research.net/index.php/fqs/article/download/ 64/131?inline=1

[34] Ryan Calo, *Artificial Intelligence Policy: A Primer and Roadmap*, 2017: https://digital commons.law.uw.edu/faculty-articles/640/

[35] The Final Report of the National Security Commission on AI, 2021: https://www. nscai.gov/

[36] See ISO/IEC 2382:2015 Information Technology Vocabulary

[37] Brad Smith and Carol Ann Browne, *Tools and Weapons: The Promise and the Peril of the Digital Age*, Penguin Press, September 2019

[38] OECD updates definition of Artificial Intelligence 'to inform EU's AI Act', November 2023: https://www.euractiv.com/section/artificial-intelligence/news/oecd-updates-definition-of-artificial-intelligence-to-inform-eus-ai-act/

[39] AI Trends Report: Industry Impact of Artificial Intelligence: https://business.bofa.com/en-us/content/ai-trends-impact-report.html

[40] Mustafa Suleyman, *The Coming Wave*, Bodley Head, 2023

[41] Two US lawyers fined for submitting fake court citations from ChatGPT: https://www.theguardian.com/technology/2023/jun/23/two-us-lawyers-fined-submitting-fake-court-citations-chatgpt

[42] Autonomous weapons that kill must be banned, insists UN chief: 25 March 2019: https://news.un.org/en/story/2019/03/1035381

[43] Hansard, House of Lords Debate on Advanced Artificial Intelligence, 24 July 2023: https://hansard.parliament.uk/lords/2023-07-24/debates/5432715E-F305-4EC1-8A79-B9A0C6402BFF/AdvancedArtificialIntelligence

[44] See in particular John Naughton, *Horrified by Horizon?* Then get ready to be totally appalled by *AI*, John Naughton, *Observer*, 14 January 2024: https://www.theguardian.com/uk-news/2024/jan/13/horrified-by-horizon-then-get-ready-to-be-totally-appalled-by-ai See Campaigners lament lack of movement on Computer Misuse Act reform, *Computer Weekly*, February 2023: https://www.computerweekly.com/news/366565613/Post-Office-scandal-furore-is-moment-to-change-digital-evidence-rules#:~:text=January%202021%3A%20Lawyers%20call%20for,price%20for%20its%20IT%20failings

[45] Frontier AI: Capabilities and risks – discussion paper: October 2023: https://www.gov.uk/government/publications/frontier-ai-capabilities-and-risks-discussion-paper

[46] EU Parliament version of the AI Act proposal agreed on 14 June 2023

[47] Taxonomy of Risks posed by Language Models, *DeepMind*, June 2022: https://dl.acm.org/doi/10.1145/3531146.3533088

[48] Global AI Safety Summit kicks off in UK with 'Bletchley Declaration': https://www.datacenterdynamics.com/en/news/global-ai-safety-summit-kicks-off-in-uk-with-bletchley-declaration/

[49] Open-Sourcing Highly Capable Foundation Models, September 2023: https://www.governance.ai/research-paper/open-sourcing-highly-capable-foundation-models

[50] Open Letter, Future of Life, March 2023, Pause Giant AI Experiments: An Open Letter: https://futureoflife.org/open-letter/pause-giant-ai-experiments/

[51] The internet was supposed to save democracy. I asked 4 tech optimists what went wrong: Dylan Matthews, Vox, June 2018: https://www.vox.com/policy-and-politics/2018/6/8/17202918/internet-democracy-facebook-cambridge-analytica-alec-ross-clay-shirky-jeff-jarvis

[52] All as described in Christopher Wylie, *Mindf*k: Inside Cambridge Analytica's Plot to Break the World*, 2019, and Anthony Barnett article describing British journalist Carole Cadwalladr's campaign to uncover the activities of Cambridge Analytica, December 2017: https://www.nybooks.com/online/2017/12/14/democracy-and-the-machinations-of-mind-control/

[53] Keynote address at Stanford University, April 2022, Democracy in the Digital Realm: https://www.obama.org/stories/democracy-challenges-2022/

[54] House of Lords Select Committee on Democracy and Digital Technologies, Digital Technology and the Resurrection of Trust, June 2020: https://publications.parliament.uk/pa/ld5801/ldselect/lddemdigi/77/7702.htm

[55] Lord Puttnam Shirley Williams Lecture on his retirement from the House of Lords, October 2021: https://www.ukpol.co.uk/lord-puttnam-2021-retirement-from-house-of-lords-speech/

[56] Facebook Hosted Surge of Misinformation and Insurrection Threats in Months Leading Up to Janary 6 Attack, Records Show, January 2022: https://www.propublica.org/article/facebook-hosted-surge-of-misinformation-and-insurrection-threats-in-months-leading-up-to-jan-6-attack-records-show

[57] Evidence of Frances Haugen to Joint Online Safety Bill Committee, 25 October 2021: https://committees.parliament.uk/oralevidence/2884/html/ and evidence to the US Senate Committee on Commerce, Science and Transportation: https://www.commerce.senate.gov/services/files/FC8A558E-824E-4914-BEDB-3A7B1190BD49

[58] Another Facebook Disinformation Election? 2019: https://secure.avaaz.org/campaign/en/disinfo_report_us_2020/

[59] Shoshana Zuboff, *The Age of Surveillance Capitalism – The Fight for a Human Future at the New Frontier of Power*, New York: Public Affairs, 2019

[60] Democracy dies without transparency and fairness, *Observer* editorial 24 March 2018: https://www.theguardian.com/commentisfree/2018/mar/24/cambridge-analytica-brexit-vote-leave

[61] House of Commons Digital, Culture, Media and Sport Committee, Disinformation and 'fake news': Final Report, February 2019: https://committees.parliament.uk/committee/378/digital-culture-media-and-sport-committee/news/103668/fake-news-report-published-17-19/

[62] Joint Committee on the Online Safety Bill, December 2021: https://committees.parliament.uk/committee/534/draft-online-safety-bill-joint-committee/publications/

[63] John Stuart, *On Liberty*, Mill, 1860

64 Article 10 of the European Convention on Human Rights: https://www.echr.coe.int/documents/d/echr/convention_eng

65 First Amendment to the US Constitution: https://constitution.congress.gov/constitution/ amendment-1/

66 Intelligence and Security Committee of Parliament, Russia, July 2020: https://isc.independent.gov.uk/wp-content/uploads/2021/03/CCS207_CCS0221966010-001_Russia-Report-v02-Web_Accessible.pdf

67 Russian Active Measures Campaigns and Interference in the 2016 US Election, volumes i-v: https://www.congress.gov/congressional-report/116th-congress/senate-report/290/1?s= 5&r=6

68 Regulating Election Finance: A review by the Committee on Standards in Public Life, July 2021: https://assets.publishing.service.gov.uk/media/ 60e460b1d3bf7f56801f3bf6/CSPL_Regulating_Election_Finance_Review_Final_Web.pdf

69 Fact Sheet on the CDU: June 2023: https://www.gov.uk/government/news/fact-sheet-on-the-cdu-and-rru

70 See in particular The Dawn of the AI Election, Tim Gordon, *Prospect* magazine, January 2024: https://www.prospectmagazine.co.uk/politics/64396/the-dawn-of-the-ai-election

71 *Economist*, November 2023: 2024 is the biggest election year in history and also see The Dawn of the AI Election, *Prospect* magazine, Tim Gordon, January 2024: https://www.prospectmagazine.co.uk/politics/64396/the-dawn-of-the-ai-election

72 AI risks undermining fabric of society, says former cyber chief, *The Times*, 8 May 2023: https://www.thetimes.co.uk/article/ai-risks-undermining-fabric-of-society-says-former-cyber-chief-wd5q2cbwl?utm_content=bufferfe1a1&utm_medium=social&utm_source=linkedin.com&utm_campaign=buffer

73 Digital propaganda revolution dominates Slovak election campaign, September 2023: https://www.intellinews.com/digital-propaganda-revolution-dominates-slovak-election-campaign-294689/

74 Deepfake audio of Sir Keir Starmer released on first day of Labour conference, 3 October 2023: https://news.sky.com/story/labour-faces-political-attack-after-deepfake-audio-is-posted-of-sir-keir-starmer-12980181 and Keir Starmer suffers UK politics' first deepfake moment. It won't be the last, *Politico*, October 2023: https://www.politico.eu/article/uk-keir-starmer-labour-party-deepfake-ai-politics-elections/

75 *Observer*, 21 January: https://www.theguardian.com/politics/2024/jan/21/call-for-action-on-deepfakes-as-fears-grow-among-mps-over-election-threat

76 Logically. AI, Actionable Intelligence: 'Detect, assess, and act on emerging threats' https://www.logically.ai/

[77] Content Authentication Initiative: https://contentauthenticity.org/

[78] Director GCHQ Sir Jeremy Fleming's full speech from the Australian National University (Thursday, 31 March 2022): https://www.gchq.gov.uk/speech/director-gchq-global-security-amid-russia-invasion-of-ukraine

[79] Blame the politicians, not the technology, for A-level fiasco: 18 August 2020: https://www.ft.com/content/58dcbfaa-740f-4747-8240-bc5ffb412e67

[80] Ada Lovelace Institute, Regulating AI in the UK: Strengthening the UK's proposals for the benefit of people and society, July 2023: https://www.adalovelaceinstitute.org/report/regulating-ai-in-the-uk/

[81] One in three councils using algorithms to make welfare decisions, *The Guardian*, October 2019: https://www.theguardian.com/society/2019/oct/15/councils-using-algorithms-make-welfare-decisions-benefits

[82] Dencik, L., Hintz, A., Redden, J. and Warne, H. (2018) Data Scores as Governance: Investigating uses of citizen scoring in public services. Research Report, Cardiff University: https://datajusticelab.org/data-scores-as-governance/

[83] Big Brother Watch, Poverty Panopticon: the hidden Algorithms shaping Britain's Welfare State, July 2021: https://bigbrotherwatch.org.uk/wp-content/uploads/2021/07/Poverty-Panopticon.pdf

[84] Child Poverty Action Group: Computer Says 'No!', July 2019: https://cpag.org.uk/sites/default/files/files/policypost/Computer%20says%20no%21%202%20-%20for%20web.pdf

[85] Statement on Visit to the United Kingdom, by Professor Philip Alston, United Nations Special Rapporteur on extreme poverty and human rights, 16 November 2018: https://www.ohchr.org/en/statements/2018/11/statement-visit-united-kingdom-professor-philip-alston-united-nations-special

[86] Home Office drops 'racist' algorithm from visa decisions: August 2020: https://www.bbc.co.uk/news/technology-53650758

[87] NYPD's Patternizr crime analysis tool raises AI bias concerns. Techtarget, March 2019: https://www.techtarget.com/searchbusinessanalytics/news/252459511/NYPDs-Patternizr-crime-analysis-tool-raises-AI-bias-concerns

[88] What happens when an algorithm cuts your health care? March 2018: https://www.theverge.com/2018/3/21/17144260/healthcare-medicaid-algorithm-arkansas-cerebral-palsy

[89] House of Lords Select Committee on Artificial intelligence 'AI in the UK: Ready Willing and Able?' April 2018: https://publications.parliament.uk/pa/ld201719/ldselect/ldai/100/100.pdf

90 Rights related to automated decision making including profiling: https://ico.org. uk/for-organisations/uk-gdpr-guidance-and-resources/individual-rights/individual-rights/rights-related-to-automated-decision-making-including-profiling/

91 Science and Technology Committee, Algorithms in Decision-Making, May 2018: https://publications.parliament.uk/pa/cm201719/cmselect/cmsctech/351/ 351.pdf

92 The Law Society: Algorithm use in the criminal justice system, June 2019: https://www.lawsociety.org.uk/topics/research/algorithm-use-in-the-criminal-justice-system-report

93 The Nolan Principles of Public Life: https://www.gov.uk/government/publications/the-7-principles-of-public-life

94 Committee on Standards in Public Life, Artificial Intelligence and Public Standards, February 2020: https://www.gov.uk/government/publications/artificial- intelligence-and-public-standards-report

95 Artificial Intelligence and Public Standards: Committee publishes report: https://www.gov.uk/government/news/artificial-intelligence-and-public-standards-committee-publishes-report

96 The EU's General Data Protection Regulation, originally adopted into UK law before exit from the EU in the Data Protection Action 2018: https://eur-lex.europa. eu/legal-content/EN/TXT/?uri=CELEX:32016R0679 and https://www.gov.uk/data-protection

97 NS Tech Exclusive: Government blocks full publication of AI review, 2 December 2019

98 A Guide to Using AI in the Public Sector, January 2020: https://assets.publishing. service.gov.uk/government/uploads/system/uploads/attachment_data/file/964787/A_ guide_to_using_AI_in_the_public_sector__Mobile_version_.pdf

99 Ethics, Transparency and Accountability Framework for Automated Decision-Making: Guidance for public sector organisations on how to use automated or algorithmic decision-making systems in a safe, sustainable and ethical way, May 2021: https://www.gov.uk/government/publications/ethics-transparency-and-accountability-framework-for-automated-decision-making

100 Equality and Human Rights Commission: Artificial intelligence: checklist for public bodies, September 2022: https://www.equalityhumanrights.com/guidance/artificial-intelligence-checklist-public-bodies-england

101 Algorithmic Transparency Recording Standard, January 2023 (updated version): https://www.gov.uk/government/publications/algorithmic-transparency-template

102 Artificial Intelligence: Public Sector: Question for Cabinet Office: https://

questions-statements.parliament.uk/written-questions/detail/2023-06-12/HL8376

[103] Directive on Automated Decision-Making, 2019: https://www.tbs-sct.canada.ca/pol/doc-eng.aspx?id=32592

[104] Institute for the Future of Work: Mind the Gap, 2020: https://www.ifow.org/publications/mind-the-gap-the-final-report-of-the-equality-taskforce#:~:text=Algorithms%20are%20increasingly%20used%20by,little%20transparency%2C%20scrutiny%20or%20accountability

[105] Justice and Home Affairs Committee: Technology Rules? The advent of new technologies in the justice system: https://publications.parliament.uk/pa/ld5802/ldselect/ldjusthom/180/18002.htm

[106] Guidelines for AI procurement: June 2020: https://www.gov.uk/government/publications/ guidelines-for-ai-procurement

[107] Procurement Act 2023: https://bills.parliament.uk/bills/3159

[108] Ada Lovelace Institute policy briefing: Foundation models in the public sector, October 2023: https://www.adalovelaceinstitute.org/policy-briefing/foundation-models-public-sector/

[109] A pro-innovation approach to AI regulation: https://www.gov.uk/government/publications/ai-regulation-a-pro-innovation-approach/white-paper

[110] Key principles for an Alternative White Paper, June 2023: https://publiclawproject.org.uk/content/uploads/2023/06/AI-alternative-white-paper-in-template.pdf

[111] Letter from Biometrics and Surveillance Camera Commissioner to Hikvision, 24 October 2023: https://www.gov.uk/government/publications/never-again-the-uks-responsibility-to-act-on-atrocities-in-xinjiang-and-beyond/letter-from-biometrics-and-surveillance-camera-commissioner-to-hikvision-24-october-2023-accessible

[112] Bridges v South Wales Police [2020] EWCA Civ 1058: https://www.judiciary.uk/wp-content/uploads/2020/08/R-Bridges-v-CC-South-Wales-ors-Judgment.pdf

[113] Report by Matthew Ryder KC commissioned by the Ada Lovelace Institute, The independent legal review of the governance of biometric data in England and Wales: https://www.adalovelaceinstitute.org/report/ryder-review-biometrics/

[114] Independent report conducted into the Met's 2019 trial of live facial recognition technology (LFR), by Professor Peter Fussey and Dr Daragh Murray of the University of Essex's Human Rights Centre: https://repository.essex.ac.uk/24946/1/London-Met-Police-Trial-of-Facial-Recognition-Tech-Report-2.pdf

[115] Operational Testing of Facial Recognition Technology, April 2023: https://science.police.uk/delivery/resources/operational-testing-of-facial-recognition-technology/

[116] Survey of Local Authorities Compliance with the Protection of Freedoms Act

2012, October 2020: https://videosurveillance.blog.gov.uk/2020/10/20/survey-of-local-authorities-compliance-with-the-protection-of-freedoms-act-2012/

[117] Joint Committee on Human Rights Oral evidence: Biometrics and Surveillance Camera Commissioner, HC 1128, Wednesday 22 February 2023: https://committees.parliament.uk/oralevidence/12717/html/

[118] UK police unlawfully processing over a million people's data on Microsoft 365: https://www.computerweekly.com/news/252493673/UK-police-unlawfully-processing-over-a-million-peoples-data-on-Microsoft-365

[119] Police use of Chinese camera tech criticised by surveillance watchdog: https://www.bbc.co.uk/news/uk-politics-64644692

[120] Data Protection and Digital Information Bill: https://bills.parliament.uk/bills/3430

[121] Centre for Research into Information Surveillance and Privacy Data Protection and Digital Information bill: addressing risks to surveillance oversight, October 2023: https://www.gov.uk/government/news/report-finds-worrying-vacuum-in-surveillance-camera-plans

[122] ICO fines facial recognition database company Clearview AI Inc more than £7.5m and orders UK data to be deleted, May 2022: https://ico.org.uk/about-the-ico/media-centre/news-and-blogs/2022/05/ico-fines-facial-recognition-database-company-clearview-ai-inc/

[123] Letter to ICO from Parliamentarians re PimEyes and Facewatch: https://bigbrotherwatch.org.uk/wp-content/uploads/2023/12/Letter-to-JE-181223-1.pdf

[124] Baden-Württemberg: LfDI Baden-Württemberg initiates proceedings against PimEyes for lack of compliance with data protection legislation: https://www.dataguidance.com/news/baden-württemberg-lfdi-baden-württemberg-initiates-0

[125] For example: Science and Technology committee: Issues with biometrics and forensics significant risk to effective functioning of the criminal justice system, July 2019: https://committees.parliament.uk/committee/135/science-innovation-and-technology-committee/news/100970/issues-with-biometrics-and-forensics-significant-risk-to-effective-functioning-of-the-criminal-justice-system/

[126] College of Policing Live Facial Recognition Authorised Professional Practice, July 2023: https://www.college.police.uk/app/live-facial-recognition

[127] Criminal Justice Bill: https://bills.parliament.uk/bills/351

[128] Pregnant woman's arrest in carjacking case spurs call to end Detroit police facial recognition, 7 August 2023: https://apnews.com/article/detroit-police-facial-recognition-lawsuitcab0ae44c1671fc3

[129] Microsoft won't sell police its facial-recognition technology, following similar moves

by Amazon and IBM, 11 June 2020: https://www.washingtonpost.com/technology/2020/06/11/microsoft-facial-recognition/

130 Rite Aid facial recognition misidentified Black, Latino and Asian people as 'likely' shoplifters, *Guardian*, 20 December 2023: https://www.theguardian.com/technology/2023/dec/20/rite-aid-shoplifting-facial-recognition-ftc-settlement

131 Ada Lovelace Institute, Countermeasures, June 2022: https://www.adalovelaceinstitute.org/report/countermeasures-biometric-technologies

132 The Minderoo Centre for Technology and Democracy, A Sociotechnical Audit: Assessing Police use of Facial Recognition, October 2022: https://www.mctd.ac.uk/a-sociotechnical-audit-assessing-police-use-of-facial-recognition/

133 Big Brother Watch, Biometric Britain, May 2023: https://bigbrotherwatch.org.uk/wp-content/uploads/2023/05/Biometric-Britain.pdf

134 Letter to Home Secretary from Baroness Hamwee, 26 January 2024: https://committees.parliament.uk/publications/43080/documents/214371/default/

135 Facial recognition cameras arrive in UK school canteens, October 17th 2021: https://www.ft.com/content/af08fe55-39f3-4894-9b2f-4115732395b9

136 North Ayrshire DPIA: https://www.north-ayrshire.gov.uk/Documents/Property Services/InfrastructureDesign/pscctv-data-protection-impact-assessment.pdf

137 House of Lords Debate on Biometric Recognition Technology in Schools: https://hansard.parliament.uk/lords/2021-11-04/debates/26FB2DF4-8D5A-456B-AFDA-73501D1CCBD3/BiometricRecognitionTechnologiesInSchools

138 See the Report on Biometric Technology in Schools from New York State's Office of Information Technology Services: https://its.ny.gov/system/files/documents/2023/08/biometrics-report-final-2023.pdf

139 Department for Education, Protection of Children's Biometric Information in Schools, July 2022: https://www.gov.uk/government/publications/protection-of-biometric-information-of-children-in-schools

140 House of Lords Liaison Committee, AI in the UK: No Room for Complacency, December 2020: https://publications.parliament.uk/pa/ld5801/ldselect/ldliaison/196/196.pdf

141 Prime Minister's Statement on progress on the Integrated Review, 19th November 2020: https://hansard.parliament.uk/commons/2020-11-19/debates/CA347B2B-EE02-40DF-B5CE-1E8FAA07139E/IntegratedReview

142 Reith Lectures 2021 – Living With Artificial Intelligence: https://www.bbc.co.uk/programmes/articles/1N0w5NcK27Tt041LPVLZ51k/reith-lectures-2021-living-with-artificial-intelligence

[143] The Integrated Review: Global Britain in A Competitive Age, March 2021: https://www.gov.uk/government/collections/the-integrated-review-2021

[144] Conference Makes No Progress on Robotic Weapons: https://www.armscontrol.org/act/2022-01/news/conference-makes-progress-robotic-weapons

[145] British Army to become force of 'boots and bots': CGS: https://www.army-technology.com/features/british-army-to-become-force-of-boots-and-bots-cgs/?cf-view&cf-closed

[146] PM to announce largest military investment in 30 years, 19 November 2020: https://www.gov.uk/government/news/pm-to-announce-largest-military-investment-in-30-years

[147] An investigation into the role of UK universities in the development of autonomous weapons systems. 2022: https://una.org.uk/KRUniReport

[148] Defence AI Strategy, June 2022: https://www.gov.uk/government/publications/defence-artificial-intelligence-strategy

[149] House of Lords oral questions, Hansard, 1 November 2021: https://hansard.parliament.uk/lords/2021-11-01/debates/8E4085C5-CA55-40C5-B218-93412DADFDB6/AutonomousWeaponsSystems

[150] Turkey's military campaign beyond its borders is powered by homemade armed drones, *Washington Post*, 29 November 2020: https://www.washingtonpost.com/world/middle_east/turkey-drones-libya-nagorno-karabakh/2020/11/29/d8c98b96-29de-11eb-9c21-3cc501d0981f_story.html and Ukraine's War Brings Autonomous Weapons to the Front Lines, Wired, 24 February 2022: https://www.wired.co.uk/article/ukraine-war-autonomous-weapons-frontlines

[151] NATO releases first-ever strategy for Artificial Intelligence, October 2021: https://www.nato.int/cps/en/natohq/news_187934.htm

[152] Ambitious, safe, responsible: our approach to the delivery of AI-enabled capability, June 2022: https://www.gov.uk/government/publications/ambitious-safe-responsible-our-approach-to-the-delivery-of-ai-enabled-capability-in-defence/ambitious-safe-responsible-our-approach-to-the-delivery-of-ai-enabled-capability-in-defence

[153] House of Lords Select Committee on AI in Weapons Systems, December 2023: https://committees.parliament.uk/publications/42387/documents/210740/default/

[154] First Committee Approves New Resolution on Lethal Autonomous Weapons, as Speaker Warns 'An Algorithm Must Not Be in Full Control of Decisions Involving Killing', November 2023: https://press.un.org/en/2023/gadis3731.doc.htm

[155] Open Letter: UK Government must ensure meaningful human control is maintained in the use of force, October 2023: https://una.org.uk/news/open-letter-uk-government-

must-ensure-meaningful-human-control-maintained-use-force

[156] *Guardian* oped 'A robot wrote this entire article. Are you scared yet, human?' 8 September 2020: https://www.theguardian.com/commentisfree/2020/sep/08/robot-wrote-this-article-gpt-3

[157] Is artificial intelligence set to become art's next medium? December 2018: https://www.christies.com/en/stories/a-collaboration-between-two-artists-one-human-one-a-machine-0cd01f4e232f4279a525a446d60d4cd1

[158] Ai-Da robot makes history by giving evidence to parliamentary inquiry, October 2022: https://www.independent.co.uk/news/uk/politics/house-of-lords-technology-liberal-democrat-b2200496.html

[159] Sony World Photography Award 2023: Winner refuses award after revealing AI creation, April 2023: https://www.bbc.co.uk/news/entertainment-arts-65296763

[160] Hollywood Actors Strike Ends With a Deal That Will Impact AI and Streaming for Decades, November 2023: https://www.wired.co.uk/article/hollywood-actors-strike-ends-ai-streaming#:~:text=WGA%20members%20went%20on%20strike,AI%20encroaching%20on%20their%20work.

[161] Directive (EU) 2019/790 of the European Parliament and of the Council of 17 April 2019 on copyright and related rights in the Digital Single Market and amending Directives 96/9/EC and 2001/29/EC: https://eur-lex.europa.eu/legal-content/EN/TXT/HTML/?uri=CELEX%3A32019L0790

[162] Creators call for Action on Copyright Exceptions, July 2023: https://graphicartistsguild.org/the-guild-joins-call-for-action-on-ai-and-copyright/

[163] Artificial Intelligence and Intellectual Property: copyright and patents: Government response to consultation, June 2022: https://www.gov.uk/government/consultations/artificial-intelligence-and-ip-copyright-and-patents/outcome/artificial-intelligence-and-intellectual-property-copyright-and-patents-government-response-to-consultation

[164] UK government bins UKIPO's flagship AI reforms: February 2023: https://www.managingip.com/article/2b8dy58efmhhbvsmaxvk0/uk-government-bins-ukipos-flagship-ai-reforms

[165] Sir Patrick Vallance's review on pro-innovation regulation for digital technologies, March 2023: https://www.gov.uk/government/publications/pro-innovation-regulation-of-technologies-review-digital-technologies

[166] Getty Images is suing the creators of AI art tool Stable Diffusion for scraping its content. *The Verge*, January 2023: https://www.theverge.com/2023/1/17/23558516/ai-art-copyright-stable-diffusion-getty-images-lawsuit

167 Microsoft, OpenAI hit with new lawsuit by authors over AI training, January 2024: https://www.reuters.com/legal/microsoft-openai-hit-with-new-lawsuit-by-authors-over-ai-training-2024-01-05/

168 Artificial intelligence and intellectual property: an interview with Francis Gurry, *WIPO Magazine*, September 2018: https://www.wipo.int/wipo_magazine/en/2018/05/article_0001.html

169 Copyright, Designs and Patents Act, 1988: https://www.legislation.gov.uk/ukpga/1988/48/contents

170 AI-created images lose US copyrights in test for new technology, February 2023: https://www.reuters.com/legal/ai-created-images-lose-us-copyrights-test-new-technology-2023-02-22/

171 US Copyright Office says some AI-assisted works may be copyrighted, March 2023: https://www.reuters.comworld/us/us-copyright-office-says-some-ai-assisted-works-may-be-copyrighted-2023-03-15/ and Copyright Registration Guidance: Works Containing Material Generated by Artificial Intelligence AGENCY: US Copyright Office, Library of Congress: Statement of policy. March 2023: https://www.federalregister.gov/documents/2023/03/16/2023-05321/copyright-registration-guidance-works-containing-material-generated-by-artificial-intelligence

172 Artificial Intelligence and Copyright: US Copyright Office, Library of Congress. Notice of inquiry and request for comments. August 2023: https://www.federalregister.gov/documents/2023/08/30/2023-18624/artificial-intelligence-and-copyright

173 Thaler v Comptroller-General of Patents, Trade Marks And Designs [2021] EWCA Civ 1374 (21 September 2021): https://www.judiciary.uk/judgments/thaler-v-comptroller/

174 Patents Act 1977: https://www.legislation.gov.uk/ukpga/1977/37/contents

175 Judgement in the Supreme Court, December 2023: https://www.supremecourt.uk/cases/uksc-2021-0201.html

176 US Supreme Court rejects computer scientist's lawsuit over AI-generated inventions, April 2023: https://www.reuters.com/legal/us-supreme-court-rejects-computer-scientists-lawsuit-over-ai-generated-2023-04-24/

177 Naming AI as inventor on patent applications: EPO Board of Appeal ratifies decision, January 2022: https://intellectual-property-helpdesk.ec.europa.eu/news-events/news/naming-ai-inventor-patent-applications-epo-board-appeal-ratifies-decision-2022-01-10_en#:~:text=According%20to%20the%20EPO%2C%20an,inventor%20on%20a%20patent%20application.

178 4 out of 5 performers don't understand their rights when working with AI,

April 2022: https://www.equity.org.uk/news/2022/4-out-of-5-performers-don-t-understand-their-rights-when-working-with-ai

[179] Stop AI Stealing the Show: https://www.equity.org.uk/campaigns-policy/stop-ai-stealing-the-show

[180] TikTok settles lawsuit with actress over its original text-to-speech voice. The Verge, September 2021: https://www.theverge.com/2021/9/29/22701167/bev-standing-tiktok-lawsuit-settles-text-to-speech-voice

[181] Beijing Treaty on Audiovisual Performances WIPO adopted on 24 June 2012, and entered into force on April 28, 2020: https://www.wipo.int/treaties/en/ip/beijing/

[182] Better Connected – Digital Britain by 2030 – Digital Skills Report March 2023: https://www.connectpa.co.uk/digital-skills-appg-materials

[183] The Future of Employment: Carl Benedikt Frey & Michael Osborne, How susceptible are jobs to computerisation?: https://www.oxfordmartin.ox.ac.uk/publications/the-future-of-employment/

[184] Technology, jobs, and the future of work, McKinsey & Co Executive Briefing, May 2017: https://www.mckinsey.com/featured-insights/employment-and-growth/technology-jobs-and-the-future-of-work

[185] AI will cost jobs on grand scale, says Bank of England chief economist, August 2018: https://www.thetimes.co.uk/article/artificial-intelligence-has-a-dark-side-andy-haldane-warns-6pbh2czw5

[186] The Risk of Automation for Jobs in OECD Countries: OECD Social, Employment and Migration Working Papers No. 189 A Comparative Analysis By Melanie Arntz (ZEW Mannheim and University of Heidelberg), Terry Gregory (ZEW Mannheim) and Ulrich Zierahn (ZEW Mannheim) 2016: https://www.oecd-ilibrary.org/social-issues-migration-health/the-risk-of-automation-for-jobs-in-oecd-countries_5jlz9h56dvq7-en

[187] Automation and the future of work – understanding the numbers, Carl Benedikt Frey and Michael Osborne of the Oxford Martin School at the University of Oxford, April 2018: https://www.oxfordmartin.ox.ac.uk/blog/automation-and-the-future-of-work-understanding-the-numbers/#:~:text=Yet%20that%20is%20not%20what,that%20existed%20in%201900%20redundant.

[188] The Future of Skills: Employment in 2030, September 2017: https://www.oxfordmartin.ox.ac.uk/publications/the-future-of-skills-employment-in-2030/

[189] Professor Richard Susskind, *The Future of the Professions: How Technology Will Transform the Work of Human Experts*, OUP Oxford; 2015. Updated edition 2022

[190] The Royal Society, Machine Learning: the power and promise of computers

that learn by example. April 2017: https://royalsociety.org/~/media/policy/projects/machine-learning/publications/machine-learning-report.pdf

[191] Growing the artificial intelligence industry in the UK, Professor Dame Wendy Hall and Jérôme Pesenti. October 2017: https://www.gov.uk/government/publications/growing-the-artificial-intelligence-industry-in-the-uk

[192] AI Roadmap, January 2021: https://www.gov.uk/government/publications/ai-roadmap

[193] Open University Skills for success: Supporting business leaders with digital adoption: https://www5.open.ac.uk/business/skills-for-success

[194] For Example, Women into Science and Engineering, The WISE Way: Delivering Women Centred Equity, Diversity and Inclusion Solutions for the STEM (Science, Technology, Engineering and Maths) Sectors: https://www.wisecampaign.org.uk

[195] The UK workforce digital skills gap. Why closing it matters and a roadmap for action. July 2023: https://futuredotnow.uk/wp-content/uploads/2023/07/FutureDotNow-roadmap_final-digital.pdf

[196] Camden STEAM Commission, Creating Camden's 21st century talent, 2017: https://www.camden.gov.uk/documents/20142/5118086/Creating+Camden's+21st+Century+Talent+-+STEAM+Commission+report%2C+June+2017.pdf/4372fc83-9f5c-6a4a-a7a9-ee79a03ed7fb

[197] We need to fill 'new collar' jobs that employers demand: IBM's Rometty, December 2016: https://eu.usatoday.com/story/tech/columnist/2016/12/13/we-need-fill-new-collar-jobs-employers-demand-ibms-rometty/95382248/ and https://s3.amazonaws.com/brt.org/ archive/IBM.2017SkillsGap.Final_.pdf

[198] Future Skills: The Kingston Approach, 2023: https://d68b3152cf5d08c2f050-97c828cc9502c69ac5af7576c62d48d6.ssl.cf3.rackcdn.com/documents/user-upload/kingston-university-83c0c7036df-kingstonreportv20digital-final-.pdf

[199] The Lifelong Learning Entitlement: https://www.gov.uk/government/publications/lifelong-learning-entitlement-lle-overview/lifelong-learning-entitlement-overview

[200] Skills for Life Campaign: https://www.gov.uk/government/collections/skills-campaign-toolkits and https://www.skillsforcareers.education.gov.uk/pages/skills-for-life

[201] Better Connected – Digital Britain by 2030 – Digital Skills Report, March 2023: https://www.connectpa.co.uk/digital-skills-appg-materials

[202] Parliamentary Office for Science and Technology (POST) Developing Essential Digital Skills: https://researchbriefings.files.parliament.uk/documents/POST-PN-0643/POST-PN-0643.pdf

[203] #StatusofMind, May 2017, https://www.rsph.org.uk/our-work/campaigns/status-of-mind.html

[204] Doteveryone: https://doteveryone.org.uk People Power and Technology, May 2017: https://doteveryone.org.uk/wp-content/uploads/2020/05/PPT-2020_Soft-Copy.pdf

[205] The Full Fact report 2021: Fighting a pandemic needs good information: https://fullfact.org/about/policy/reports/full-fact-report-2021/

[206] Ofcom Report on Adults' Media Use & Attitudes report 2020 Cited in DCMS Online Media Literacy Strategy, July 2021: https://www.gov.uk/government/publications/online-media-literacy-strategy

[207] Online media literacy: Across the world, demand for training is going unmet, March 2021: https://www.ipsos.com/en-uk/online-media-literacy-across-world-demand-training-going-unmet

[208] Online Safety Act: https://www.legislation.gov.uk/ukpga/2023/50/enacted

[209] Communications Act: https://www.legislation.gov.uk/ukpga/2003/21/contents

[210] House of Lords Communications and Digital Committee Free for all? Freedom of expression in the digital age, July 2021: https://committees.parliament.uk/publications/6878/documents/72529/default/

[211] Government response to the House of Lords Communications Committee's report on Freedom of Expression in the Digital Age, October 2021: https://committees.parliament.uk/publications/7704/documents/80449/default/

[212] Media Literacy Strategy and Framework: https://assets.publishing.service.gov.uk/media/60f6a632d3bf7f56867df4e1/DCMS_Media_Literacy_Report_Roll_Out_Accessible_PDF.pdf

[213] All-Party Parliamentary Group on Media Literacy Research into the current media literacy landscape in England, April 2022

[214] Over a third of parents have children with no exclusive use of a device to work from home, February 2021: https://www.teachfirst.org.uk/press-release/ongoing-digital-divide

[215] Data Poverty, APPG, August 2023: https://www.datapovertyappg.co.uk/news/the-data-poverty-appgs-second-state-of-the-nation-report and House of Lords Communications and Digital Committee Digital Exclusion, June 2023

[216] UK Consumer Digital Index: https://www.lloydsbank.com/banking-with-us/whats-happening/consumer-digital-index.html

[217] Ofcom Adults' Media Use and Attitudes Report, 2022: https://www.ofcom.org.uk/__data/assets/pdf_file/0020/234362/adults-media-use-and-attitudes-report-2022.pdf

[218] Good Things Foundation Evidence to House of Lords Communications and Digital Committee: https://committees.parliament.uk/writtenevidence/119049/html/ and CEBRExecutive Briefing, The Economic Case for Digital Inclusion 2022: https://www.goodthingsfoundation.org/wp-content/uploads/2022/07Good-Things-Foundation-and-CEBR-2022---Executive-Summary.pdf\

[219] The role of councils in tackling digital exclusion, Local Government Association, January 2023: http://www.local.gov.uk/publications/role-councils-tackling-digital-exclusion

[220] Government Digital Inclusion Strategy, December 2014: https://www.gov.uk/government/publications/government-digital-inclusion-strategy/government-digital-inclusion-strategy

[221] 100% Digital Leeds: https://digitalinclusionleeds.com/

[222] Greater Manchester Combined Authority/Stockport Homes October 2023: https://www.greatermanchester-ca.gov.uk/news/uk-s-biggest-social-housing-digital-inclusion-pilot-makes-positive-steps-towards-tackling-the-digital-divide/

[223] Gig Rights & Gig Wrongs Initial Findings from the Gig Rights Project: Labour Rights, Co-Determination, Collectivism and Job Quality in the UK. Gig Economy, May 2023: https://papers.ssrn.com/sol3/papers.cfm?abstract_id=4446226

[224] Foxglove Briefing: Busting Amazon's myths about its unsafe warehouses and management by algorithm. Evidence to BEIS Select Committee as part of its inquiry into AI and technology in the Workplace, December 2022: https://committees.parliament.uk/written evidence/114223/pdf/

[225] The New Frontier: Artificial Intelligence at Work November 2021: https://www.ifow.org/publications/new-frontier-artificial-intelligence-work

[226] Teresa May, Davos World Economic Forum Speech; PM's speech at Davos, 25 January 2018: https://www.gov.uk/government/speeches/pms-speech-at-davos-2018-25-january

[227] Industrial Strategy: building a Britain fit for the future, November 2017: https://assets.publishing.service.gov.uk/media/5a8224cbed915d74e3401f69/industrial-strategy-white-paper-web-ready-version.pdf

[228] The Centre for Data Ethics: https://www.gov.uk/government/organisations/centre-for-data-ethics-and-innovation

[229] OECD AI Principles Overview, May 2019: https://oecd.ai/cn/ai principles

[230] G20 AI Principles: https://www.mofa.go.jp/policy/economy/g20_summit/osaka19/pdf/documents/en/annex_08.pdf

[231] Recommendation on the Ethics of Artificial Intelligence, UNESCO 2021: https://unesdoc.unesco.org/ark:/48223/pf0000381137

232 G7 Leaders' Statement on the Hiroshima AI Process, October 2023: https://www.mofa.go.jp/ecm/ec/page5e_000076.html

233 International Guiding Principles for Organizations Developing Advanced AI Systems and Code of Conduct: https://www.mofa.go.jp/files/100573471.pdf and https://www.mofa.go.jp/files/100573473.pdf

234 Microsoft's CEO Calls for Accountable AI, Ignores the Algorithms That Already Rule Our Lives, June 2016: https://www.technologyreview.com/2016/06/29/70696/microsofts-ceo-calls-for-accountable-ai-ignores-the-algorithms-that-already-rule-our-lives/

235 Evidence to House of Lords AI Select Committee, Corrected oral evidence: Artificial Intelligence, Tuesday, 17 October 2017: https://data.parliament.uk/writtenevidence/committeeevidence.svc/evidencedocument/artificial-intelligence-committee/artificial-intelligence/oral/71898.html

236 Proposal for a Directive of the European Parliament and of the Council on adapting non-contractual civil liability rules to artificial intelligence (AI liability directive), September 2022: https://eur-lex.europa.eu/legal-content/EN/TXT/?uri=CELEX%3A52022PC0496

237 Partnership on AI: https://partnershiponai.org

238 Empowering AI Leadership: AI C-Suite Toolkit, January 2022: https://www.weforum.org/publications/empowering-ai-leadership-ai-c-suite-toolkit/ And World Economic Forum World Economic Forum Launches AI Governance Alliance Focused on Responsible Generative AI, June 2023: https://www.weforum.org/press/2023/06/world-economic-forum-launches-ai-governance-alliance-focused-on-responsible-generative-ai/

239 Singapore's Approach to AI Governance: https://www.pdpc.gov.sg/Help-and-Resources/ 2020/01/Model-AI-Governance-Framework

240 Corporate Ethics in a Digital Age, Board briefing, June 2019: https://www.ibe.org.uk/resource/corporate-ethics-in-a-digital-age.html

241 New technologies, ethics and accountability, ICAEW, 2019: https://www.icaew.com/-/media/corporate/files/technical/technology/thought-leadership/new-technologies-ethics-and-accountability.ashx

242 World Economic Forum Insight Report. The AI Governance Journey: Development and Opportunities, October 2021: https://www3.weforum.org/docs/WEF_The%20AI_Governance_Journey_Development_and_Opportunities_2021.pdf

243 Also see IOD Model Artificial Intelligence Governance Framework, January 2020: https://www.pdpc.gov.sg/-/media/files/pdpc/pdf-files/resource-for-organisation/ai/sgmodelaigovframework2.pdf

[244] Voluntary AI Commitments, July 2023: https://www.whitehouse.gov/wp-content/uploads/2023/09/Voluntary-AI-Commitments-September-2023.pdf and White House Fact Sheet Biden-Harris Administration Secures Voluntary Commitments from Eight Additional Artificial Intelligence Companies to Manage the Risks Posed by AI, September 2023: https://www.whitehouse.gov/briefing-room/statements-releases/2023/09/12/fact-sheet-biden-harris-administration-secures-voluntary-commitments-from-eight-additional-artificial-intelligence-companies-to-manage-the-risks-posed-by-ai/

[245] Hollywood Writers Reached an AI Deal That Will Rewrite History, Wired, September 2023: https://www.wired.com/story/us-writers-strike-ai-provisions-precedents/ and Hollywood Actors Strike Ends With a Deal That Will Impact AI and Streaming for Decades, Wired, November 2023: Hollywood Actors Strike Ends With a Deal That Will Impact AI and Streaming for Decades | WIRED

[246] The BBC is blocking OpenAI data scraping but is open to AI-powered journalism. The Verge, October 2023: https://www.theverge.com/2023/10/6/23906645/bbc-generative-ai-news-openai

[247] The Associated Press sets AI guidelines for journalists: https://www.theverge.com/2023/8/16/23834586/associated-press-ai-guidelines-journalists-openai

[248] For Example: Guidance on how to prepare a user policy on generative AI for your workplace and how this technology can be used to support HR functions, CIPD, June 2023: https://www.cipd.org/uk/knowledge/guides/preparing-organisation-ai-use/

[249] Sir Ronald Cohen: The Impact Revolution | CogX 2020: https://www.youtube.com/watch?v=0HHgZDeMVEs

[250] Also Integrated Corporate Governance: A Practical Guide to Stakeholder Capitalism for Boards of Directors, June 2020: https://www.weforum.org/publications/integrated-corporate-governance-a-practical-guide-to-stakeholder-capitalism-for-boards-of-directors/

[251] The Big Innovation Centre, The Purposeful Company policy. February 2017 report: https://thepurposefulcompany.org/wp-content/uploads/2021/01/feb-24_tpc_policy-report_final_printed-2.pdf and https://thepurposefulcompany.org/

[252] The B Corp movement: https://www.bcorporation.net/en-us/

[253] For an excellent overview comparing approaches see Rules to keep AI in check: nations carve different paths for tech regulation, Matthew Hutson, Nature, August 2023: https://www.nature.com/articles/d41586-023-02491-y#:~:text=08%20August%202023-,Rules%20to%20keep%20AI%20in%20check%3A%20nations%20carve%20different%20paths,are%20reining%20in%20artificial%20intelligence.&text=Matthew%20

Hutson%20is%20a%20science%20writer%20based%20in%20New%20York%20City

[254] Artificial Intelligence for Europe, April 2018: https://eur-lex.europa.eu/legal-content/EN/TXT/?uri=COM:2018:237:FIN

[255] High-level Expert group on Artificial Intelligence Ethics, Guidelines for Trustworthy AI, 2019: https://digital-strategy.ec.europa.eu/en/library/ethics-guidelines-trustworthy-ai

[256] Artificial intelligence act: Council and Parliament strike a deal on the first rules for AI in the world: https://www.consilium.europa.eu/en/press/press-releases/2023/12/09/artificial-intelligence-act-council-and-parliament-strike-a-deal-on-the-first-worldwide-rules-for-ai/

[257] National Artificial Intelligence Initiative Act of 2020: https://www.congress.gov/bill/116th-congress/house-bill/6216

[258] Blueprint for an AI Bill of Rights, Making Automated Systems Work for the American People, October 2022: https://www.whitehouse.gov/wp-content/uploads/2022/10/Blueprint-for-an-AI-Bill-of-Rights.pdf

[259] Executive Order on Safe, Secure, and Trustworthy Artificial Intelligence, October 2023: https://www.whitehouse.gov/briefing-room/presidential-actions/2023/10/30/executive-order-on-the-safe-secure-and-trustworthy-development-and-use-of-artificial-intelligence/

[260] US senators introduce bill to create framework to support AI transparency, accountability, November 2023: https://iapp.org/news/a/us-senators-introduce-bill-to-create-framework-to-support-ai-transparency-accountability/

[261] The Office for AI Guide to using AI and Procurement Guidelines, June 2020: https://assets.publishing.service.gov.uk/media/60b356228fa8f5489723d170/Guidelines_for_AI_procurement.pdf

[262] Various publications from the CDEI: https://www.gov.uk/government/publications/cdei-ai-barometer and https://www.gov.uk/government/publications/cdei-publishes-review-into-bias-in-algorithmic-decision-making

[263] Explaining decisions made with AI, ICO, October 2022: https://ico.org.uk/for-organisations/uk-gdpr-guidance-and-resources/artificial-intelligence/explaining-decisions-made-with-artificial-intelligence also https://ico.org.uk/media/for-organisations/guide-to-data-protection/key-dp-themes/explaining-decisions-made-with-artificial-intelligence-1-0.pdf

[264] The Ethics of Artificial Intelligence, GCHQ, 2021: https://www.gchq.gov.uk/artificial-intelligence/index.html

[265] National AI strategy, September 2021: https://www.gov.uk/government/

publications/national-ai-strategy

266 The roadmap to an effective AI assurance ecosystem, December 2021: https://www.gov.uk/government/publications/the-roadmap-to-an-effective-ai-assurance-ecosystem

267 National AI Strategy – AI Action Plan, July 2022: https://www.gov.uk/government/publications/national-ai-strategy-ai-action-plan/national-ai-strategy-ai-action-plan

268 AI Governance White Paper: A pro-innovation approach to AI regulation, August 2023: https://www.gov.uk/government/publications/ai-regulation-a-pro-innovation-approach/white-paper

269 Regulating AI in the UK: Strengthening the UK's proposals for the benefit of people and society, July 2023: https://www.adalovelaceinstitute.org/report/regulating-ai-in-the-uk/

270 Science, Innovation and Technology Committee, August 2023: https://publications.parliament.uk/pa/cm5803/cmselect/cmsctech/1769/report.html

271 An Ethical AI Future: Guardrails and Catalysts to Make Artificial Intelligence a Force for Good Policy Connect and the All Party Parliamentary Group on Data Analytics, June 2023: https://www policyconnect.org.uk/research/ethical-ai-future-guardrails-catalysts-make-artificial-intelligence-force-good (inquiry cochaired by the Author)

272 Digital Regulation Cooperation Forum (DRCF): https://www.ofcom.org.uk/about-ofcom/how-ofcom-is-run/organisations-we-work-with/drcf

273 Common Regulatory Capacity for AI, July 2022: https://www.turing.ac.uk/news/publications/common-regulatory-capacity-ai

274 ICO Guidance and Resources: Rights related to automated decision-making including profiling: https://ico.org.uk/for-organisations/uk-gdpr-guidance-and-resources/individual-rights/individual-rights/rights-related-to-automated-decision-making-including-profiling

275 Data Protection and Digital Information Bill: https://bills.parliament.uk/bills/3430

276 House of Commons Science and Technology Committee: Algorithms in Decision-Making, May 2018: https://publications.parliament.uk/pa/cm201719/cmselect cmsctech/351/351.pdf

277 Equality and Human Rights Commission Briefing on House of Lords Second Reading of the Data Protection and Digital Information Bill, December 2023: https://www.equalityhumanrights.com/our-work/advising-parliament-and-governments/data-protection-and-digital-information-bill-house-0

278 The Global Partnership on Artificial Intelligence: https://gpai.ai

279 Launching The AI Standards Hub: The new home of the AI standards community,

October 2022: https://www.turing.ac.uk/events/launching-ai-standards-hub

280 An Ethical AI Future: Guardrails and Catalysts to Make Artificial Intelligence a Force for Good, Policy Connect and the All-Party Parliamentary Group on Data Analytics, June 2023: https://www.policyconnect.org.uk/research/ethical-ai-future-guardrails-catalysts-make-artificial-intelligence-force-good (Inquiry cochaired by the Author)

281 ISO/IEC 42001:2023: https://www.iso.org/standard/81230.html NIST, A Risk Management Framework, January 2023: https://www.nist.gov/itl/ai-risk-management-framework and IEEE, 7000™-2021 Standard: https://engage standards.ieee.org/ieee-7000-2021-for-systems-design-ethical-concerns.html

282 Human Rights, Democracy, and the Rule of Law Impact Assessment: https://rm.coe.int/huderaf-coe-final-1-2752-6741-5300-v-1/1680a3f688

283 Common Guideposts to Promote Interoperability in AI Risk Management, OECD Artificial intelligence Papers, November 2023: https://www.oecd-ilibrary.org/docserver/ba602d18-en

284 We have put the world in danger with artificial intelligence, admits ChatGPT creator, Telegraph, 16 May 2023: https://www.telegraph.co.uk/business/2023/05/16/chatgpt-creator-sam-altman-admits-world-in-danger/

285 The Sprawl Trilogy, William Gibson Ace 1984–88: https://en.wikipedia.org/wiki/Sprawl_trilogy

286 Big Tech stocks' massive gains this year have made them even more dominant. That could be bad news for investors. Business Insider, May 2023: https://markets.businessinsider.com/news/stocks/big-tech-stocks-apple-microsoft-alphabet-amazon-nvidia-meta-charts-2023-5#:~:text=Stock%20market%20vulnerability,more%20reliant%20on%20borrowing%20cash.

287 Challenge to Google is a sign of fights to come, September 23rd: https://www.thetimes.co.uk/article/challenge-to-google-is-a-sign-of-fights-to-come-npk0l2rj3

288 Metcalfe's Law: https://en.wikipedia.org/wiki/Metcalfe%27s_law

289 Ex-post Assessment of Merger Control Decisions in Digital Markets, Lear, May 2019: https://assets.publishing.service.gov.uk/media/5ce54e9aed915d2475aca875/CMA_past_digital_mergers_GOV.UK_version.pdf

290 Unlocking Digital Competition Report of the Digital Competition Expert Panel, March 2019: https://assets.publishing.service.gov.uk/media/5c88150ee5274a230219c35f/unlocking_digital_competition_furman_review_web.pdf

291 Power to the People John Penrose MP, February 2021: https://assets.publishing.service.gov.uk/media/602aa137d3bf7f0314acbfd7/penrose-report-final.pdf

[292] Digital Markets Unit: https://www.gov.uk/government/collections/digital-markets-unit

[293] Google, Facebook and Amazon face new UK regulator, April 2021: https://www.bbc.co.uk/news/technology-56648922

[294] The Digital Services Act package: https://digital-strategy.ec.europa.eu/en/policies/digital-services-act-package

[295] Facebook, Inc., In the Matter of, December 2023: https://www.ftc.gov/legal-library/browse/cases-proceedings/092-3184-182-3109-c-4365-facebook-inc-matter

[296] Microsoft's Activision Blizzard deal approved by UK regulators, October 2023: https://www.theverge.com/2023/10/13/23796552/microsoft-activision-blizzard-cma-approval-uk

[297] Ofcom refers UK cloud market to CMA for investigation, October 2023: https://www.ofcom.org.uk/news-centre/2023/ofcom-refers-uk-cloud-market-to-cma-for-investigation

[298] CMA launches initial review of artificial intelligence models, May 2023: https://www.gov.uk/government/news/cma-launches-initial-review-of-artificial-intelligence-models and CMA AI Foundation Models Initial Report, September 2023: https://assets.publishing.service.gov.uk/media/65081d3aa41cc300145612c0/Full_report_.pdf

[299] Open Markets Institute: November 2023, AI in the Public Interest: Confronting the Monopoly Threat: https://www.openmarketsinstitute.org/publications/report-ai-in-the-public-interest-confronting-the-monopoly-threat

[300] UK says first in G7 to ratify China-backed development bank, December 2015: https://www.reuters.com/article/britain-asia-bank-idINL8N13S3S520151203/

[301] https://www.thetimes.co.uk/article/revealed-how-china-is-buying-up-britain-t7njdhhc5

[302] UK Trade and investment core statistics, December 2023 book: https://www.gov.uk/government/statistics/trade-and-investment-core-statistics-book/trade-and-investment-core-statistics-book

[303] Full Translation: China's 'New Generation Artificial Intelligence Development Plan' (2017): https://digichina.stanford.edu/work/full-translation-chinas-new-generation-artificial-intelligence-development-plan-2017/

[304] Who Is Winning the AI Race: China, the EU, or the United States? – 2021 Update: https://itif.org/publications/2021/01/25/who-winning-ai-race-china-eu-or-united-states-2021-update/ and Europe holds its own in supercomputer race as China squeezes out US, January 2022: https://sciencebusiness.net/news/europe-holds-its-own-supercomputer-race-china-squeezes-out-us

305 The Geopolitics of digital standards China's role in Standards Setting Organisations, December 2021: https://www.diplomacy.edu/wp-content/uploads/2021/12/Geopolitics-of-digital-standards-Dec-2021.pdf

306 Sale of 3Com to Huawei is derailed by US security concerns, February 2008: https://www.nytimes.com/2008/02/21/business/worldbusiness/21iht-3com.1.10258216.html Huawei ends fight against CFIUS ruling on 3Leaf acquisition February 2011: https://www.lexology.com/library/detail.aspx?g=72c39543-03d4-4365-bb98-44cf491b9862

307 Biden asks G-7 to take a tougher line on China, but not all allies are enthusiastic: https://www.washingtonpost.com/politics/g7-biden-china/2021/ 06/12/532a0bb2-cb66-11eb-a11b-6c6191ccd599_story.html

308 White House Fact Sheet: President Biden and G7 Leaders Launch Build Back Better World (B3W) Partnership, June 2021: https://www.whitehouse.gov/briefing-room/statements-releases/2021/06/12/fact-sheet-president-biden-and-g7-leaders-launch-build-back-better-world-b3w-partnership/

309 The National Security Commission on Artificial Intelligence Report, March 2021: https://reports.nscai.gov/final-report/

310 Chips and Science Act: https://www.congress.gov/bill/117th-congress/house-bill/4346

311 Made in China 2025: https://www.csis.org/analysis/made-china-2025

312 National Security and Investment Act 2021: https://www.legislation.gov.uk/ukpga/2021/25/contents/enacte

313 Telecommunications (Security) Act 2021: https://www.legislation.gov.uk/ukpga/2021/31/contents/enacted

314 Global Britain in a Competitive Age: the Integrated Review of Security, Defence, Development and Foreign Policy, March 2021: https://www.gov.uk/government/publications/global-britain-in-a-competitive-age-the-integrated-review-of-security-defence-development-and-foreign-policy

315 For example: MI5 boss says 'tens of thousands' of UK companies at risk from Chinese AI threat, October 2023: https://news.sky.com/story/mi5-boss-says-tens-of-thousands-of-uk-companies-at-risk-from-chinese-ai-threat-12986152 and Chinese technology poses major risk – GCHQ Chief October 2022: https://www.bbc.co.uk/news/uk-63207771

316 The National Cyber Security Centre: https://www.ncsc.gov.uk/

317 Advanced Research and Invention Agency: https://www.aria.org.uk/

318 Building Resilient Supply Chains, Revitalising Manufacturing and Fostering Broad-based Growth June 2021: https://www.whitehouse.gov/wp-content/

uploads/2021/06/100-day-supply-chain-review-report.pdf

[319] EU and China reach agreement in principle on investment, December 2020: https://ec.europa.eu/commission/presscorner/detail/en/ip_20_2541

[320] EU parliament 'freezes' China trade deal over sanctions, May 2021: https://www.theguardian.com/world/2021/may/20/eu-parliament-freezes-china-trade-deal-over-sanctions

[321] EU slams China's 'authoritarian shift' and broken economic promises, April 2021: https://www.politico.eu/article/eu-china-biden-economy-climate-europe/

[322] G7 urged to take 'allied action' against China on artificial intelligence, quantum and 5G, January 2021: https://sciencebusiness.net/news/g7-urged-take-allied-action-against-china-artificial-intelligence-quantum-and-5g

[323] EU, US tech relations get a photo opp boost, but will this build the digital society we want or just the one we deserve? June 2021: https://diginomica.com/eu-us-tech-relations-get-photo-opp-boost-will-build-digital-society-we-want-or-just-one-we-deserve

[324] The Fight for Digital Sovereignty: What It Is, and Why It Matters, Especially for the EU, August 2020: https://link.springer.com/article/10.1007/s13347-020-00423-6

[325] Beijing AI Principles, May 2019: https://link.springer.com/content/pdf/10.1007/s11623-019-1183-6.pdf

[326] China's New AI Governance Initiatives Shouldn't Be Ignored: January 2022: https://carnegieendowment.org/2022/01/04/china-s-new-ai-governance-initiatives-shouldn-t-be-ignored-pub-86127

[327] China says to set governance rules for algorithms over next three years, September 2021: https://www.reuters.com/world/china/china-says-set-governance-rules-algorithms-over-next-three-years-2021-09-29/

[328] China bans AI-generated media without watermarks, December 2022: https://arstechnica.com/information-technology/2022/12/china-bans-ai-generated-media-without-watermarks/

[329] How to Interpret China's First Effort to Regulate Generative AI Measures, July 2023: https://www.china-briefing.com/news/how-to-interpret-chinas-first-effort-to-regulate-generative-ai-measures/

[330] Oliver Dowden says Britain must work with China over AI. *The Times*, 29 September 2023: https://www.thetimes.co.uk/article/oliver-dowden-says-britain-must-work-with-china-over-ai-sgn8wszd2

[331] The Institute for Ethical AI in Education, Developing the Ethical Framework for AI in Education: https://www.buckingham.ac.uk/research/research-in-applied-

computing/the-institute-for-ethical-ai-in-education/

[332] Algorithmic impact assessment: a case study in healthcare, February 2022: https://www.adalovelaceinstitute.org/report/algorithmic-impact-assessment-case-study-healthcare/

[333] Ben Dellot RSA, A Hippocratic Oath for AI developers? It may only be a matter of time: https://www.ukauthority.com/articles/a-hippocratic-oath-for-ai-developers-it-may-only-be-a-matter-of-time/

[334] The International Association of Privacy Professionals: https://iapp.org/ and https://iapp.org/about/ai-governance-center/

[335] The Bletchley Declaration by Countries Attending the AI Safety Summit, 1–2 November 2023: https://www.gov.uk/government/publications/ai-safety-summit-2023-the-bletchley-declaration/the-bletchley-declaration-by-countries-attending-the-ai-safety-summit-1-2-november-2023

[336] Guy Davenport, *The Fragments of Heraclitus and Diogenes*, Grey Fox Press 2001: https://blogs.baruch.cuny.edu/authenticityandastonishment2/files/2013/02/Guy-Davenport-The-Fragments-of-Heraclitus-and-Diogenes.pdf

[337] Brad Smith and Carol Ann Browne, *Tools and Weapons: The Promise and the Peril of the Digital Age*, Penguin Press, September 2019

INDEX